The Divine Comedy

ACADEMIC PURGATORY

Stuck in the Middle

The Divine Comedy

ACADEMIC PURGATORY

Stuck in the Middle

Virgil Henry

Accomplishing
Innovation Press

DEDICATION

For the true believers
Don't stop

TABLE
OF CONTENTS

DEDICATION V

INTRODUCTION IX
    ANTE-PURGATORY

PETER'S GATE 1

PRIDE 7

ENVY 14

WRATH 21

SLOTH 28

GREED 36

GLUTTONY 43

LUST 53

THE EARTHLY PARADISE 61

BOOK CLUB QUESTIONS 69

AUTHOR BIO 71
    VIRGIL HENRY

INTRODUCTION

Ante-Purgatory

O Ye whose end was good,
O now elected spirits, by peace,
Which I believe, ye all look forward

Dante's Purgatory Canto III

WELCOME BACK. IF YOU'VE NOT READ THE FIRST book in this trilogy, you should. It was pretty good. As good as the OG Dante's *Inferno?* Who's to say? My book was an allegory just like the original. My version was in English, and it had a lot of swearing, modern-day technology, and relatable ideas to the modern reader. Dante's was an epic poem written in Italian. I don't read Italian, and odds are you don't either, so really it all comes down to the translation, doesn't it? That isn't to say you couldn't be fluent in Italian, but the odds are against it. There are what, 7 plus billion people in the world, and around 65 million of them speak Italian[1], so there you go.

Anyway, people seemed to like it. Professors in particular loved it. One person said she was considering getting into adjuncting for some extra cash, read the book, and decided that staying in a library was a better idea. For sure. Unfortunately, libraries have all kinds of political bullshittery going on, some of that will likely come up here, and if someone were so inclined, one could easily write a library Inferno. Really, anyone could write an Inferno about

---

[1] "Italian - Worldwide Distribution." *Worlddata.Info*, www.worlddata.info/languages/italian.php. Accessed 8 June 2024.

anything. Fast food Inferno would be interesting. Customer service is a nightmare, so any of those jobs could be infernoized. I just made that word up. Let's make it happen, people. #infernoized. I would love to see that trending.

Of course, some hated it. Some people hate everything. Don't believe me? Go to Goodreads and look up your favorite book; someone has written an absurd one-star review of it. I recently saw a one-star review of a book that the person admitted to having never read. I would give that review no stars if I could. Fuck that guy. It wasn't even my book, but still, don't be a dick. The people whom I suspect disliked my book and who will dislike this book and will be annoyed when the third book comes out (I've already sold the trilogy, fuckers!!) will be college administrators. There is no doubt that administrators hate-hated it. An extra hate for the extra pain it caused. The truth hurts, baby. The truth hurts.

So, I'm back, and if you are reading this, it means you, too, are back for more. If you are new, and you've had the warning about going back and reading the first book, hello, thanks for going to read that first book. What did you think? Feel free to leave a review on Goodreads[2]. Any stars are good as long as you've read it. I mean, you don't want to be a dick, do you?

In the first book, I talked shit about book two of the original trilogy. Look, I wasn't saying it was bad; I was saying most people don't read it in school. Teachers don't assign the middle book by itself. *Purgatory* is a classic middle book in a trilogy. Dante didn't invent the trilogy, so he can't take credit for that, but he did lay some groundwork. You start with the characters from the first book, and then you give them a moment to breathe before you make them do some more crazy shit that either advances the plot or undoes everything that happened in the first one. While the latter seems like it is counterproductive, it isn't. Growth happens when we realize we made a mistake and that we have to make a move. I had a full-time job, which I quit. I currently have a full-time job,

2 "Academic Inferno: My Academic Trip through Adjunct Hell." *Goodreads*, www.goodreads.com/book/show/210447768-academic-inferno. Accessed 8 June 2024.

and I am open to leaving and working somewhere else. Some of the reasons why will be evident soon enough.

Think of it this way. When you get a haircut that you hate, you are not stuck with it forever. You can wear a hat or a wig or never leave the house until it grows back to the way you used to have it. When you go into a clothing store, you can try things on. You change your clothes. Then you see yourself in it and decide if it is good, and if not, you change back. Clothing stores are places that sell items that are real and that you can touch and feel with your hands, not some stupid VR goggles that some tech bro wants to make happen. It isn't going to happen, bro. Let it go. Besides, you missed the point on *Snow Crash*.[3]

Purgatory is essentially a place to wait and think about "what you've done." It is like a cosmic time-out or a waiting room or trying to switch planes in Atlanta. It seems endless, and you will never get out, and you maybe pray to your deity for forgiveness, and you promise never to do that bad thing or come to the DMV at noon on a Tuesday or have connecting planes in Atlanta again. Seriously, what the fuck, Atlanta? You have trains that connect two sides of the same fucking terminal. That means it isn't a terminal as much as it is in a different part of a city. That is how trains work. Fuck.

Anyway, Purgatory isn't the same thing as a purgatorium, which you are mistaking for a vomitorium, that place where Romans puked after binge eating. It doesn't actually matter because those are fiction.[4] Yes, your dad, uncle, or grandpa told you some story about it when you were a kid, but what did that guy know? Really? How many things did he lie about or just simply make up? The list is long, isn't it? You may have read about them in *The Hunger Games*, but those too, as of now, are also fiction. Unless this book has survived into the future, and you are a survivor of whatever war it was that the Capital had with the districts, then that is a fact. All hail President Snow.

3   Stephenson, Neal. *Snow Crash*. Milano, Rizzoli, 1992.

4   Pappas, Stephanie. "Purging the Myth of the Vomitorium." *Scientific American*, www.scientificamerican.com/article/ purging-the-myth-of-the-vomitorium/.

In the book, Dante and Virgil (no relation) leave Hell and discover that they are at the center of the Earth, and there are dinosaurs! What? Amazing. Is that Brendon Fraser over there? He was so good as George of the Jungle. Just kidding. They do discover some fresh air though. Hell is supposed to be just below Jerusalem, so it is sort of the center of the Earth, and there is a little place to hang out and have some water and then have a sit and a think and a chat and some reflection on what they just went through, all while looking up at Purgatory Mountain because, of course, purgatory is a mountain. If it was an easy-going paved road with guard rails and road stops, it wouldn't be a challenge, and it wouldn't be "worth it." So, after they do all of that, because it is *that* kind of sequel, they choose to climb back up because they are told Paradise is at the top. On Easter Sunday, no less. So much for having time off. On a holiday. Blasphemy. If they weren't already in Hell, that could be a big problem.

Just like them, my journey here begins with me being settled into my job. I'm in the ante-purgatory. The room outside the room. I get why it was called ante-purgatory in the 14th century, but no one says anteroom anymore. Is it purgatory's vestibule? The foyer? Hmmm. As good luck would have it, I am writing this chapter on Easter weekend. Divine intervention? No, but still, an amazing coincidence.

Either way, this is where my journey and this collection begins. I'm no longer doing the part-time work. I've landed the full-time job that was supposed to be the last job I will ever need. I've become a traitor against my adjunct brethren, and to get there, I went through hell, worked on holidays, fought the baddies, froze, sweated, got kicked in the metaphorical balls, and I have decided to take a break and see what I want to do next.

I had some choices. I could have sat still and just sort of done the job as it came to me. I could have kept my head down. There is a way for me to realistically do almost nothing to draw attention to myself. I can choose to make no waves and hold down a chair for the next 30 years. That is what a lot of people do. There are some valid reasons for that. We shall explore those here in this collection. It is easy to do and hard to resist. The pay is good. The job is not physically demanding. It beats a lot of alternatives. I know. I've done a lot of the alternatives.

Option two was to start pouring the kerosene to just see the place burn because breaking things and being evil is fun. Seems like a horrible thing to do, but let's be honest, we all know those people. They are the absolute fucking worst. They will show up here. How could they not? There are times when we all have to resist the urge to light the match. That's the thing, though: we resist. Maybe some people think this book is the match or the kerosene, or someone will use this book to light a fire. Two things: 1. Don't burn books. Just don't. 2. Pointing out flaws isn't destructive. Just because the world seems to have become binary and either you are for something or against something, that isn't true. The truth is a little more nuanced than that, and this book, like the one that came before and the one that will come after, is about facing the truth, not burning things down.

Finally, and I am not saying there are only three choices, there are always more, but we are sticking with these three: I could choose to get involved and to help make the place I work grow and change for the better. No place is perfect, is it? Certainly not. However, if behind door one is a snow plow that will run me over, door two hides the keys to the snow plow that I can use to run people over, and door three has some gloves and a toque and shovel, I choose door three.

PETER'S GATE

Perhaps this bird is wont to strike but here,
And from elsewhere, perhaps,
Disdains to lift one with its claws

Dante's Purgatory Canto IX

SURPRISED TO BE AT PETER'S GATE DOWN here? Yeah. No shit. What are the logistics of that? Like, if I go straight to heaven, is he there too? Do I wake up dead in between the edge of Hell and the foot of Mt. Purgatory, and then I'm judged, and if I don't have to deal with all this shit, there's like an elevator? Best not to think about it too hard, really.

So, what do we know about St. Peter and his Gate? How did he get to be the judge? Does that mean he like doesn't get to go to Heaven either, but he sort of sits outside of the gates forever while looking at everyone going in? Does he have regular business hours? He is the Patron Saint of Fishermen (Fisherwomen and Fisherpeople who are non-binary are likely covered but don't hold me to that. I can say with confidence he is not the Patron Saint of Fisher Price Little People. That's Andy), so maybe he works Fisherman hours and shows up around 5 and knocks off for the day around 2 or 3. Regardless, the thing about Peter's Gate isn't the location or hours of operation; it is the meaning. This is an allegory after all.

Having left a high-paying, tenure-track job for a lower-paying, at-will job wasn't much of a choice for me. The people at that other job sucked sweaty balls, and they liked it. I'm not here to kink shame or anything about sucking on balls be they dry or sweaty, but making a commentary about them being terrible people and thus, there will be a lot of ball sucking references here. If you would prefer it said more directly, those people were assholes. Maybe I have some strange kind of unbridled optimism, but when I started the new job, the forever job as I thought of it, I was sure the bullying and thus all the judgment was over. I thought everyone would be on the same page.

When I first started the forever job, there was even a yearly retreat where the faculty, the staff, and the administrators in my division got together for the day and had a big party. There was eating, drinking, and merry-making. Newbies had a chance to mingle with the veterans. If friendships were not formed, at least there was some kind of mutual respect. We ended the party by singing and doing a choreographed dance to "We're All in This Together[5]" from *High School Musical*, which is objectively catchy and absurdly positive. I stopped and listened to it just now, and wow, that is going to be stuck in my head for the next forty days. If you know the song, or if you clicked on the link in the footnote, it will be wormed into your ear as well. You're welcome. Anyway, back in reality, we were singing and dancing, and we even swapped out "Wildcats" with the name of our college's mascot. I could be misremembering the whole thing too. The boss paid for a full bar, so anything is possible.

Of course, unbeknownst to me, the moment I stepped foot on campus that year, I approached Peter's Gate, and the judgment began. Unfortunately for me, there wasn't just one giant Peter, who sat erect on firm stones, to judge me for things I have done or not done. Instead, there were a whole bunch of dicks who flopped over, sitting on soft cushions, whispering mean things based on what they assumed I was doing or not doing. (Side note: I accidentally typed "dong" instead of doing at first. Is there such a thing as too many dick jokes?) The problem was that, due to all the singing and dancing and Wildcat chanting, I didn't recognize what was going on until it was too late.

There is a saying about never having a second chance to make a first impression. I didn't bother to find out who said it because no one cared. I would take umbrage with the idea that one can't

---

5 DisneyMusicVEVO. "High School Musical Cast - We're All in This Together (from "High School Musical")." *YouTube*, 22 Aug. 2019, youtu.be/ DykVJl6wr_4?si=XPDQI_b82a9RVQUT.

overcome a bad first impression. Of course, we can, it just takes a lot of work, and college Professors are notorious for being lazy as fuck. This comes from making choices early on and picking one of the three doors mentioned in the introduction. Again, not everyone. I'm not lazy. I picked door three. I know at least a dozen people who are working today, and it is Easter Sunday. If a person is or is not a Christian and works in higher ed, Sunday is still Sunday. It should be a day off, right? And one shouldn't be working or feeling guilty about not working on one's day off.

Granted, that isn't a conversation about laziness as much as it is about the pressure one feels to constantly work, and so it is one of the many conundrums that come with working in higher education and how the way we are judged in the first year we work somewhere determines the path we follow. Work your ass off or be a lazy ass? Is a lazy ass an ass that sort of hangs and is saggy? Better to have a saggy, hanger-on ass than no ass at all? The problem is that no matter what one chooses, one is judged harshly for it, and thus, one finds oneself at a Citgo late at night filling a can with kerosene while opening and closing the lid on a Zippo and muttering things under one's breath.

I try hard not to judge people too quickly, but of course, I do. I am human. Humans do bad shit. Look around wherever you are; there is some bad shit happening right now because of humans. We are flawed, but we have thumbs and feet, and so here we are. Take that, dolphins. Still, besides my casual dolphinism, I do try my best to be a good person. I genuinely walked into my new job so happy to be away from the bullies and the bullshit. I knew a few people when I first arrived on campus, but determined to branch out, I sat down at a random table with a bunch of people I didn't know. Mistake.

Yeah. If you started singing Bowling for Soup's "High School Never Ends[6]" just now, then you get it. If you didn't, go listen. There's a link just down there (Thanks, Laura, for thinking of adding footnotes. Editors for the WIN!). The group in question

---

[6] BowlingForSoupVEVO. "Bowling for Soup - High School Never Ends (Official Music Video)." *YouTube*, 25 Oct. 2009, youtu.be/jrxI_euTX4A?si=VQtOdHI_RhxyLaA3.

were, and this is true and can only exist as the set up to a bad joke or on a college campus, a nurse, a philosopher, a literature scholar, and a political scientist. They all had doctorates, yep, even the nurse, because a doctorate of nursing[7] is a thing. Suck that you doctors of medicine with all of your high-and-mighty "the nurse can't do that" bullshit. Nurses "can do that" AND can be doctors.

It was innocent enough when I sat down. We shook hands and introduced ourselves. I explained I was new and was happy to be there, which I was. I found out who they were, what they taught, and how long they'd been at the college. We chatted about the food and the campus and the parking, and it was all nice. I'd just met these people, so really, it should have stayed nice. Yet, by the time I stood up from that lunch, three of them actively disliked me, and my relationship with them was tenuous at best and downright hostile at worst. The fourth person and I were in the same department, so it could be that she was decent because she was stuck working with me, or it could be that she just agreed. I don't know. She was quiet, decent, and I thought very hardworking. She has since left the university, and so we shall never know if she secretly hated me too. I didn't come in covered in dolphin blood while wearing a dolphin fin around my neck. I hadn't stolen anyone's job. I didn't slash any tires. What I did do was have an opinion that went against the hive mind. Gasp.

Another old-timey saying is that opinions are like assholes; everyone has one. I try to keep that in mind, but sometimes, the person *is* an asshole so… yeah. I honestly have no idea how we ended up moving from all the nice stuff to faculty workload, but once we moved there, things went sideways. I thought that being a faculty member was a challenging, difficult, but rewarding job. Having grown up without a lot of academic role models, as no one in either generation above me went to college, I thought working for a college was sort of like being on an extended vacation. I showered in the morning, not at night. If I hurt my fingers while at work, it was from slamming them in a door or a hole-punching

---

[7] "About the Doctor of Nursing Practice (DNP)." *Www.aacnnursing. org*, July 2023, www.aacnnursing.org/our-initiatives/education-practice/ doctor-of-nursing-practice/about-the-dnp.

incident. To that end, I thought I was being well-paid for the work I was being asked to do, and thus, I didn't mind coming in with big ideas of how I could contribute. I was youngish. I was in my 40s and could, in theory, spend the next 30 years being part of this community of people who wanted to serve the students.

Wrong answer. The philosopher said that the college was ripping us off, and we should all be paid at least double. The political scientist said that we needed to unionize. The nurse agreed. The nurse, by the way, was making more than anyone at the table because to get nurses to teach, especially Dr. nurses, they need to be paid industry money, which is, well, way more than a philosopher makes. If everyone else knew that at the time, I don't know. Shakes a magic 8 ball. Signs point to no. Hmmm. I didn't know until much, much later, and it was only because my boss let it slip or said it out of anger or both.

I countered with the fact that I'd just left a union job and had a terrible experience. I said that while unions do a lot of good, they actually can get in the way of the students. It was, and is, my opinion that teaching is a service job. People who have something to give to others, in our case, have expertise and wisdom that we hope to impart to the next generation. Service jobs never pay as well as non-service jobs. Facts. Capitalism feeds itself. Sure, do I wish I were paid more? Yes. However, I took a pay cut to come from the union job and landed the forever job because I thought this place had a student-first mission whereas the union job had a teacher-first vibe. Teaching, I pointed out, is not about the money. If we wanted to be rich, we wouldn't have become academics… right? I paused for laughter. No one laughed.

That was it. That was the great mistake I made on day one. Day. One. I didn't know about the doors yet. They hadn't materialized. I just, like Dante and other Virgil, came through Hell and thought everything was going to be OK. I didn't know there was a whole new trial waiting for me. I didn't realize that I was in the middle part of a trilogy. I thought I was in the epilogue, and it was going to read, "And he served his students and college with pride and lived happily ever after in obscurity. The end." Instead, I was just at the beginning. I left that lunch and walked out and saw before me a whole new problem. I sat judged by Peter. None of them were named Peter, but they were, for the most part, a bunch of dicks.

PRIDE

That Teacher,
Which toward us I see advancing
Does not look like people,
Nor know I what, my sight is so deceived

Dante's Purgatory Canto X

OKAY, LOOK, I FUDGED A BIT WITH THE WAY I broke that line up there. Call it artistic license if you will. The word "Teacher" is capitalized because Dante is talking to Virgil who is, and of course, this is intentional, a teacher. Depending on the translation, there is a comma after the word "that." It changes everything, doesn't it? Punctuation matters. "We ate, Grandma" is way different than "We ate Grandma." Yikes, didn't expect cannibalism to make an appearance. Anyway, the way I did it makes it seem that the teacher coming toward us does not look human anymore, and that is the point here.

Pride can be seen in one of two ways; in both ways, it alters the person considerably. The first, and the one most people think of, is the idea of vanity. Vainglorious people will do all kinds of extreme things to themselves. Yes, I know extreme is a relative term. All things are relative. I get it. I say extreme; you say it is perfectly normal that Michael Jackson looked the way he did at the end of his life. Noses fall off all the time[8].

When we think of vanity in that way, we think of the physical changes, and those are easy to see. That lady looks like a cat or that guy's eyebrows are suddenly really angry or that individual wanted

---

8 ABC News. "Surgeon: Michael Jackson a 'Nasal Cripple.' *ABC* News https://abcnews.go.com/Health/Cosmetic/story?id=131910&page=1

us to see a full set of teeth all the time. Cool, cool, cool. You do you, but I'll age like a person ages and deal with a wrinkle or a crow's foot or some neck jiggling. You rub that leather protector on your face like it is a saddle.

The second way that pride changes a person is on the inside. This doesn't mean the person suddenly had five hearts or four uteruses (uteri?). It just means the person changes how s/he/y acts due to an emotional shift. If you are say, dead inside, you will likely act like a zombie. If you are a hateful spite-filled megalomaniac, you might run for president and try to destroy your country from the inside out. Generally, pride manifests itself when a person draws some imaginary line in the sand or builds a hill upon which s/he/y is willing to die for honestly arbitrary reasons that are likely self-serving, stupid, and built on a mountain of lies. Yes, there is sand and a hill on this mountain. Lots of metaphors happening here. I could use some other trite phrases people say, but it all comes down to someone saying, "I won't ever…" This is a fill-in-the-blank, not an ellipsis, in that I will tell you the rest. You fill in the blank. What have you said, "I won't ever…" to at work or in life? Why did you say it? Upon what was it based? Did you back down? Why or why not? Find a partner and discuss. I'll wait. Back? Good. Let's move on.

Folks who let pride take over their lives may not be easy to understand for those who don't do this. It might seem to you that binding your feet is bad for your physical health or becoming so intractable that you ostracize everyone you know is bad for your mental health. Both are true. People do shit that is bad for them all the time. People are, as a group, dumb. Don't be offended. I am people too. So why is this? What does it all come down to? Why would someone cut off one's nose to spite one's face (both literally and metaphorically)? It is my contention that pride in either form (and let's face it, there are more, but this book is short, and we are only on chapter 3 here) all comes down to being afraid.

Fear is a huge dick. As I discussed in my previous book, fear makes people do a lot of things that they wouldn't do when not in a heightened state. I know because I was afraid and on edge and I've snapped at people I love or strangers or that one annoying as fuck co-worker; Steve had it coming. He always pushed my buttons. Steve. There's always a fucking Steve. STEVE!!

What was I talking about? Right? Sorry. Fear and pride. Go ahead and do a quick search in your favorite search engine about the connection between pride and fear, and you will find oodles of articles as well as a lot of religious commentary on how pride and fear sit next to each other on the emotional bus. Buddhists, Christians, Jews, and likely everyone else agree. People let pride get in the way because they are afraid. Jews even consider pride the root of all evil. Wow. That seems extreme but maybe.

These religious folks all go on with some spiritual hoo-ha, and I'm not going to do that. Mostly because I am not remotely qualified to speak at length about religiosity. Sure, I am an academic and an above-average researcher, but still, I will stay in my lane here. I don't even like saying "bless you" when people sneeze. I don't even bless myself when I walk into a building of worship; why would I think I have the right and/or power to bless someone for sneezing? Also, why is it only when we sneeze? We make other sounds that could indicate we are sick. A hacking cough for instance is more of a red flag about one's health than, say, a reaction to having too much of one spice in a meal. Maybe that only happens in cartoons. Regardless, we are not going down that rabbit hole.

The point is a person yelled at Steve, got a facelift, or decided s/he/y would never do that thing ever because s/he/y was terrified. That person was scared that Steve had a point, that s/he/y might look less attractive, or that s/he/y might agree with someone s/he/y knows has a different political or ethical point of view. Instead of trying to grow from that, that person's pride got in the way, and s/he/y shit h/i/r metaphorical pants or maybe even h/i/r actual pants. Don't be ashamed. It happens.

In academia, people are not super worried about what they look like. I mean, we've all seen a Professor rock up to class in shorts, socks, and Birkenstocks. I had a Professor who showed up, and this is true, in his robe. He lived across the street, and he was always running late. Dude, why the fuck did you schedule this class for 8 in the goddamn morning if you can't fucking make it? I'm a teenager, and I am here, not in my robe or jammies, but in my outside pants and outside shoes and shirt that I didn't sleep in the night before. I'm paying a lot of money for this class. Could you at least, I don't know, brush your fucking teeth or at least your hair? No? This isn't remotely distracting at all. I guess this is how we learn now.

While these folks don't care what they look like, they care what they "look like" or, that is to say, how they seem to others, and this is how the second part of pride gets in the way. For whatever reason, lots of people in higher ed, the people who've been tasked to teach the next generation of great thinkers, are closed-minded, defensive narcissists. They don't want to seem weak or wrong or wishy-washy or some other word that starts with "w," so they decide to take firm stands, and this can, and often does, create chaos.

Teaching is all about learning. Every day I walk into the classroom or log into an online discussion board, I expect to learn something new. It could be something simple about a particular student, something that will come in handy later when I am helping that student pick a topic for a paper, or it could be some historical or cultural fact I simply didn't know because the world is full of shit I don't know. I love it. I love to learn. I love not knowing something so that later, I can know it. It is one of the best parts of my working days. Lots of teachers end up on *Jeopardy* for this very reason. They learn from their students.

Those of us who not only don't care what we look like (I've taught a class in a t-shirt with a cereal mascot on it) or don't care how we seem to others find joy in the work. The act of teaching is an act of service. Sure, I'm being paid for the service. Granted, I am not paid well, but I am doing something that hopefully helps the greater good. I am not teaching a firefighter how to put out a fire, but I am teaching h/i/em to write a report that will allow h/i/em to be a chief. I'm not teaching a nurse how to take someone's blood pressure, but I am helping h/i/em learn how to research so s/h/ey can earn an LNP degree and diagnose an illness. I don't teach the skill; I teach other things that have value.

See, I am proud of the job I do. I do good work, and of that I am proud. Many of my colleagues are proud of themselves too. I am proud of them. I know that the work I did with them is good.

I know that every day I learn from my students and I learn from my colleagues too. That is a good thing. It is hard to admit that we are good at things, but I am good at teaching, and I am proud of that. However, I know I have a lot to learn. I know my lessons can be cleaned up. I know I can make positive changes. I can write a course and have feedback from a colleague and understand they are not trying to stick me with an emotional shiv, except for Steve. Fucking Steve.

It isn't a job that people are supposed to take if they are egomaniacs. Unfortunately, earning a terminal degree and being called Professor, Doctor, Dean, or President, feeling proud can suddenly turn into pride because people are afraid of being shivved by Steve. So, even though s/he/y's worked hard getting the job and getting where s/he/y wanted to be, s/he/y forgot what it was s/he/y was even doing. S/he/y gets to be in charge now, so s/he/y gets to make proclamations and decrees and fire people or change policy or do whatever the fuck s/he/y wants just because s/he/y can because S/he/y's the boss now. S/he/y's proven h/i/emself. S/he/y is the supreme ruler, and at some point, s/he/y forgot that s/he/y didn't achieve greatness all alone. It's like s/he/y pretends s/he/y's never had any help or that s/he/y's never collaborated.

So, once someone has created a version of the truth that is total bullshit, it is hard to see reality. Everything becomes a personal attack, and so s/he/y takes perceived attacks and responds with actual attacks. If someone were to suggest that s/he/y try something new or, and this happens all the time, that someone else try something new, s/he/y freaks the fuck out. Especially when the person wants to try something new in a course or program that the supreme ruler designed or led. S/he/y then chooses not to act like a person who has earned one of those titles or who has years and years of extensive high-level academic training but instead, like a toddler having a meltdown.

Recently, I've run into plenty of on-ground faculty who are unwilling to allow the courses they oversee to be taught online. Keep in mind several things here. First, no one is asking THAT person to teach the course online but just suggesting that the course be offered online by someone else. Secondly, no one is suggesting that on-ground courses are garbage. I mean, some of them are, but so are some online courses; some people just suck at teaching or course design or both. Remember having a PhD in math doesn't mean you can teach math. It means you can learn math. Finally, in this day and age (whenever you are reading this, unless Snake Plissken ended all technology like he seemed to do at the end of *Escape From L.A*[9], we can assume the internet still exists), students want to have the option to take online courses. Not all of them do, but many do. At the beginning of 2024, the majority of them do[10].

So again, no one is making anyone do anything. People are just trying to offer choices to students in different modalities, but because one person doesn't want to, it doesn't happen. Some excuses are "Students can't learn that way" or "Students don't like it." As reported in the cited article from the previous paragraph, the fact remains that students do want the online option. It is just an option, remember? There is no decree; there is just an option. There are thousands of scholarly articles that prove students can learn that way. NOT ALL students do, but they can and it is effective[11].

Higher ed has this strange "Only I can do that" mentality and that too comes down to fear-based pride. I mean, unless the teacher comes back from the future *Looper* style and teaches himself (The people who object the hardest in my personal experience are almost always a him, and he is almost always white) his subject matter at the school where he currently teaches, then it is obviously false. I learned from great teachers, who learned from great teachers. I teach one way, but someone else teaches the same subject in a different and hopefully effective way. Again, some people suck and some people are amazing, and believe it or not, some people are both. Crazy, I know, but it is true. Facts.

---

[9] *Escape From LA*. Directed by John Carpenter. Paramount Pictures. 1996.

[10] Peck, Devlin. "Online Learning Statistics: The Ultiamte List in 2024." *Devlin Peck*. https://www.devlinpeck.com/content/online-learning-statistics.

[11] University of Washington. "Asynchronous learning." *Teaching@ UW*. https://teaching.washington.edu/course-design/flipped-hybrid-and-online-teaching/asynchronous-learning/.

I will be honest: I didn't expect stonewalling and bullshit at this level. I thought people became educators because they cared, but that turned out to be false. There is an old adage that says, "Those who can't do, teach." Maybe that is the big secret. Someone wanted to be a great actor but didn't get a break, so that person became a bitter acting Professor or math Professor or history Professor (You get it).

The solution isn't easy. Students have a lot of power here. They need to fill out those faculty evaluations. Shitty teachers need to be called out. Good teachers need to be praised. Maybe if the good ones get the promotions and the awards and the recognition, then the shitty ones will swallow all that pride and compromise. We can only hope because we know the future of the world depends on the next generation being well-educated enough to fix the shit we broke.

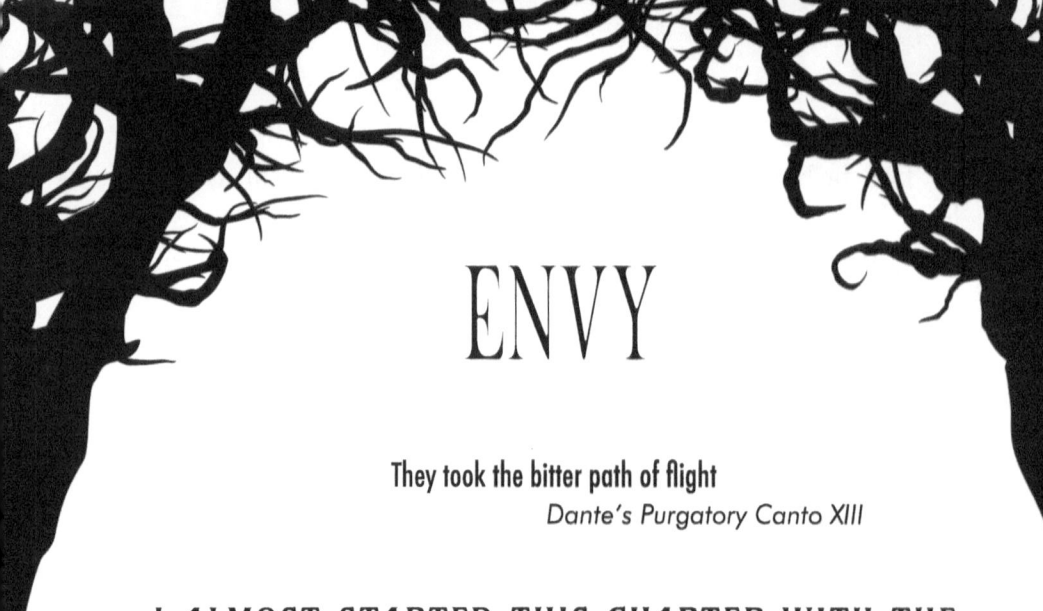

ENVY

They took the bitter path of flight
Dante's Purgatory Canto XIII

I ALMOST STARTED THIS CHAPTER WITH THE quote, "They have no wine!" I mean, there is nothing more disappointing than showing up somewhere expecting an open bar and ending up with a flat RC Cola or some room-temperature melon water. People, stop putting melon in water. No one wants that. Lemons. Yes. Limes. Sure. Cucumbers… maybe. Melons? What the fuck? It only is worse when you see someone over there, likely Steve, drinking the last bit of the whiskey or wine or beer or whatever it is you want. He doesn't even want it; he is just holding it and letting it get warm in his damp, dead-fish hands. Fuck you, Steve. Either drink it or pour it out, but don't do that.

While we may be envious of Steve and his drink, we can understand that. He has a thing we thought we would get, and it was arbitrary that he got the last one and we didn't. While we might be annoyed for a while or start chapter four of an essay collection about it, for the most part, we let it go. Most envy is short-lived. They were out of Double Stuff Oreos, and you had to settle for regular Stuff. You'll live. You wanted to get front row seats, but you had to settle for second row. That's fine. Still great seats. The front row is so 1990s anyway. Another team picked up the free agent you hoped your team would pick up. That is sucky. Boo! In three weeks, you are cheering for that other player your team picked up instead, who is obviously better than that other chump anyway. Good luck with that loser! We rule.

As I've established, higher ed isn't like the rest of the world. It should be like the rest of the world because it is a place where people are trained to be in the world but, alas, no. Academia is a place where people have a LOT of time on their hands to sit around and be petty. This time is factored into a Professor's contract. When on campus, faculty members are required to be available for office hours. I went into this in the first book, but it is worth a quick reminder here as I want to look at office hours from a different perspective. It is generally one hour per 3-credit course. Most faculty teach four to five 3-credit courses per semester, so for four to five hours per week, they are contractually obligated to sit in their office space and "be available." Most Professors grade assignments or work on something else, but in theory, they could be interrupted at any time by a student in need, so it is hard to get into anything too deeply. However, because most students don't know what office hours are[12] or what purpose they serve, students don't come. Still, during weeks when nothing is due to be graded, Professors sit and wait and hope to be useful, or if the person is Steve, he hopes to have the chance to mansplain something to a young person. Thus, with all that free time, these Professors sit and stew in a pot of envy. Envy stew smells as bad as it sounds.

Folks who work at colleges are not as collegial as they should be, even though the root of the word is right there. Academic jealousy is a real thing. There are plenty of studies on it. Here is one[13]. Here is a confessional[14]. That person even calls it "Academic Envy," so… yeah. I guess you should just read those, and we can call this chapter done, huh? Please don't. I mean, please read them. I found hundreds. The problem is real. People are the worst.

---

[12] Smith, Margaret, et al. *"Office Hours Are Kind of Weird": Reclaiming a Resource to Foster Student- Faculty Interaction.* Vol. 12, 2017, files.eric.ed.gov/fulltext/EJ1152098.pdf.

[13] Bayar, Adem, and Mehmet Koca. "The Perspectives of Academicians on Academic Jealousy." *Shanlax International Journal of Education*, vol. 9, no. 4, 1 Sept. 2021, pp. 78–90, https://doi.org/10.34293/education.v9i4.4064.

[14] "The University of Chicago Magazine." *Mag.uchicago.edu*, mag.uchicago.edu/arts-humanities/academic-envy.

The system is set up to make us compete with each other. I've been teaching for 30 years and was named employee of the month twice, and I've been the "Teacher of the Year" twice in all that time. Oddly enough, I was not given the Teacher of the Year award in either of the years when I was named Employee of the Month. Each time I was honored, it was an award where the nominations came from students and were decided upon by my colleagues (there's that root word again). I have been nominated more times than I won. I was given a nomination just this month by the chair of a search committee on which I served. I mean, that person nominated us all because being on a search committee sucks Steve's sweaty balls. To be fair, I don't have first-hand knowledge about the condition of Steve's balls, but balls get sweaty sometimes, so it is safe to assume. If anyone should win the Employee of the Month award this month, it should be the person who chaired that committee. I can assume that sucked both dry and sweaty balls.

Does that mean during my 30-year teaching career, I was busy arbitrarily giving grades while napping in my office? It does not. I just keep going about my job because I like my job, despite what this essay collection seems to say. I just want my school to be a nice place for the faculty, staff, and students. I want to work hard and do good work. If I'd never been nominated for the awards, I would have worked just as hard. I was nominated for the awards and won them because I didn't seek them out. I am not competitive, and in academia, it makes me a bit of a unicorn.

In an "industry" that doesn't "make" anything, words matter. Teachers can't show off the latest car they built or the house they built or the... well anything they've built. Thus, titles, degrees, awards, and publications all matter. They matter so much that people get incredibly pissy about it. Some Professors get so jealous when someone else gets published or earns a new degree that they will actively try to keep each other down in other ways. Getting published or earning a new degree are things people generally take on in their own time, although some people get paid by the university to do personal work. There is nothing someone like say, Steve, can do to stop me from publishing this book (suck it, Steve), and so people like him and his ilk will engage in Academic Sabatoge ™ (capitalized here as though it is a real thing, but I just made it up).

Academic Sabotage takes many forms. In simple terms, people will not vote for someone to get a promotion. Rank and promotion aren't rewarded on merit. That would make a lot of sense. It should go like this:

Hey Virgil, I see you have been working your ass off and not just assigning grades at random. I've noticed your students seem to learn things, they seem to like you, you've chaired a committee, presented at that conference, AND you served on that one committee over and above while also writing this book. Good job. Promotion!

That is not remotely how it goes. Instead, there is a long, arduous process and the final decision comes down to a committee of peers. It is essentially an Academic Body Cavity Search ™. It is simple enough to serve on the Rank and Promotion Committee and cast a "nay" vote while working hard to convince the rest of the committee to do the same. It is a shitty thing to do, but since serving on that committee is more painful and awful than going through the aforementioned process, not many people want to do it. So once there, in that position of power, already having earned the highest rank, that person will sit forever and ever, passing judgment and keeping people down.

There are lots of options for the chair with all the power to be a huge dick. S/he/y can flood the pool of the Teacher of the Year award with a bunch of nominees, thus ensuring the pool is diluted and making it harder for the deserving person to win. The list is long. If you could think of something some jealous asshole could do, it has likely been done. Was the show *Survivor* inspired by academia? Maybe.

The thing that fucking pisses me off is the dreaded whisper campaign. They are so easy to start and virtually impossible to stop once they begin. Whisper campaigns are lies told anonymously to as many people as possible. Because people are gullible and prone to believe something they've heard over and over, even if it isn't true, these campaigns can destroy someone's reputation. It is called the Illusory Truth Effect[15]. It is a level of bullshittery that is almost impossible to come back from because once someone believes something, s/he/y won't change h/i/r mind even when presented with facts.

There is a guy I work with who is admittedly a difficult grader. He has high standards. He has a ton of degrees. He speaks at conferences. He has written books. He is the real deal. He worked his way up from obscurity. He is a bootstrapper in the truest sense, not in the "poor people just need some bootstraps and they will be fine" way. That is also a myth. This guy from work had help. He earned scholarships. He applied for grants. He had advisors and Professors who believed in him. They pushed him. They were hard on him. Not in an abusive way. They told him when his shit wasn't good enough and that he had to do better.

He feels that being treated that way got him to his position, and so he treats his students that way. He feels that grade inflation is trash and that if students want top marks, they need to earn those marks. A isn't for effort in his class; A is for mastery of material. That is actually what earning an A is supposed to mean. We don't live in that world anymore, and when we get to book 3, I have a lot to say about how to deconstruct grades. When I take over the educational world, things will change for the better. Promise. It will be a real *Paradise*. That's foreshadowing. You have to finish this book and then wait a year or just keep reading if you are holding the collected edition sometime in the future. For now, though, we live in this world, and I teach at this school where this guy pushes his students.

Keep in mind that this guy admits to being a hard grader. He owns it. Still, his classes are always full, and students seem to like him. What does that do to the Professor who can't get h/i/r classes filled even though everyone gets an A? What does s/he/y think when s/he/y sits alone in h/i/r office, waiting for h/i/r students to come and ask questions? S/he/y thinks s/he/y needs to get the hard-grading Professor out of there. S/he/y needs to get him fired. S/he/y needs him to be taken down a thousand pegs because

---

[15] The Decision Lab. "Illusory Truth Effect - the Decision Lab." *The Decision Lab*, 2018, thedecisionlab.com/biases/illusory-truth-effect.

instead of doing the work to be liked by students by having high standards while making the material interesting and fun, the thing to do is to make shit up about him so that students will stop taking his classes, and he will not be a threat any longer. I have heard that he grades on a curve so that someone always fails his classes no matter what grade s/he/y earns. Even if the lowest grade is 88 percent, that person will fail. That is a thing some people do; it is not a thing the hard grader does. No one at my school does this. It is a shitty thing to do, and it should stop wherever it is done. Keep in mind it isn't done here at my school by him or anyone. Yet enough people have said it about him that it got back to me. I wasn't asking. It just sort of came up in conversation because that is how whisper campaigns work.

There is one floating around about him not grading the papers at all but just giving out grades and playing favorites. Not true at all, but it leads to the worst of the worst of the fucking worst. Did you guess it? Yep. The rumor is that he is a racist. Not just any old racist. Not just old-fashioned *Dukes of Hazzard* racism. This guy, who is a person of color, is racist against other people of color. He isn't racist against white people, which some people call "reverse racism," which isn't a thing, and "some people" should shut their fucking mouths and stop repeating bullshit, which is, of course, the whole point of this section. Snake eats tail and all of that.

Where was I? Right, the person of color who hates other people of color because of… jealousy. That's right. He is jealous of these teenagers who are just at the beginning of their college journey while he just spoke at a conference last week in front of thousands of people and has two books coming out next year. He's jealous. He's threatened. Really? Really, really? Come on. There is no way anyone should possibly believe that, and yet I've heard it, so at least one person believes it.

I actively dislike a lot of people, but I would never do this. I would never and have never spread a rumor about a colleague. I would never and have never spread truths about a colleague. I don't talk about them with colleagues or students. I don't even talk about my own books and my own personal shit. Why would I talk about anyone else's? This isn't middle school. We don't tattle.

Sure, if someone is doing something illegal or unethical, I will turn that person in. I have done this. Often it leads nowhere, but I did the work. I did it by the book. I have called HR on a colleague for whom I was worried. I thought his mental health was fragile, and I wanted him to get help. I could have gotten on a text chain and called people and said, "Did you hear about…?" Instead, I had conversations with people who were also concerned about him, and then I told the HR director in confidence about my concerns.

In the above case, I was concerned about my colleague, and I was concerned about his students. The times I reported workplace bullying, when I was the target of the bullying, I did it because I wanted my school to be a nice place for everyone. I wanted that then, and I want that now. I know that we need a team of good, solid, competent people who can do good work. I'm not envious of someone who gets a promotion that they earned. I'm not upset when someone becomes chair of a department because s/he/y wants the job. I might get angry when a person who doesn't deserve it or who fails up gets the job (more on that in the next chapter), but I'm not jealous. I'm not envious.

Envy gets us nowhere. It is a drag. It is an anchor that keeps us down, and that is why so many Professors are stuck at this level of the mountain of Academic Purgatory. They can't admit that they could get better while other people also get better. They think, wrongly, like other wrong-headed buffoons, that they alone can fix it. I know that I can't do it alone. I know I didn't get here alone, and I know that people are better than me at a lot of things, so instead of getting weighed down by this shit anymore, I am going to drop anchor and get climbing. Wrath is up ahead, and boy am I pissed.

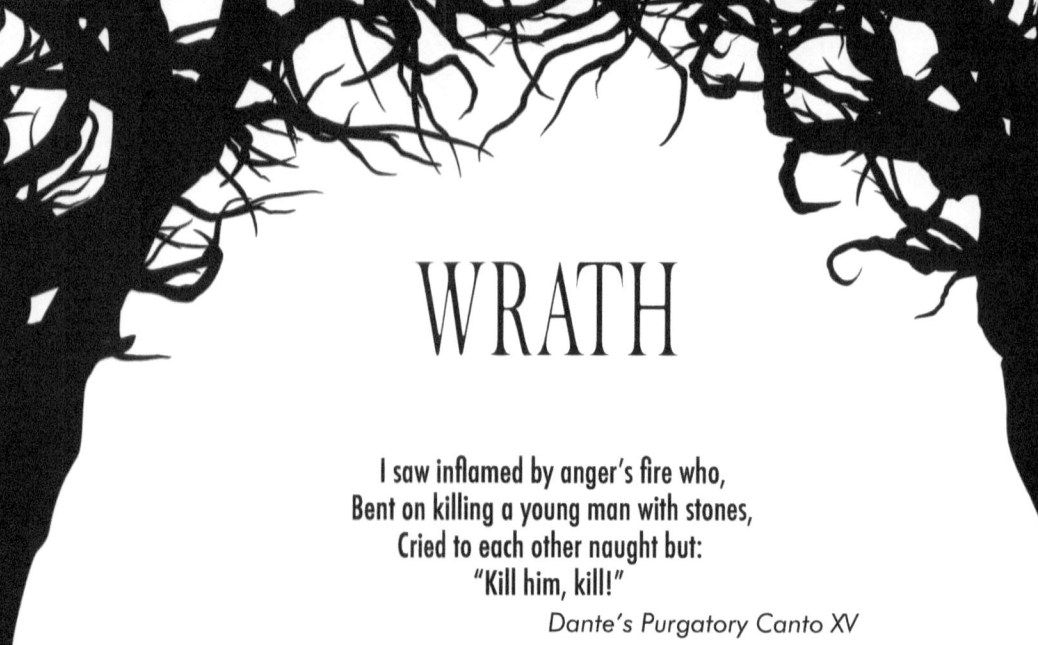

WRATH

I saw inflamed by anger's fire who,
Bent on killing a young man with stones,
Cried to each other naught but:
"Kill him, kill!"

Dante's Purgatory Canto XV

I HATE TO ADMIT IT, BUT I AM TRYING TO BE A

reliable narrator here, but this is where I am right now. As I write this, I am sitting one-third of the way up the mountain, which is not quite halfway through this book, and I am so enraged that I fear I can't climb up any farther. I mean, the book isn't going to end here. I just feel that, for me, as I sit in Academic Purgatory, I'm weighed down by anger. It is all-consuming. When I wake up in the middle of the night, I think about work and not in a good way. When I tell stories about work, they are all bad. I have good students who are doing amazing things, but all I can think about is how furious I am about something or other. Keep in mind that I have done a ton of jobs that were not teaching while I was trying to become a full-time teacher. While I felt a lot of wrath at the circumstances that kept me from getting the gig, I never really felt the kind of full-bodied misery that I feel right now.

Just the other day, I was sitting on the couch at the end of a random Thursday when my body sort of became jelly. I'd been carrying around a knot in between my shoulder blades for, I'd say, three years, and on that day, shortly after dinner, when I sat down, cocktail in hand, to watch some sitcom that had been canceled years before, it all just went away. My shoulders dropped. The tension moved through my body, and I could feel it in my legs. I needed to use the side of the couch to stand up. I was shaky on my feet like I was drunk, but the cocktail wasn't that strong at all. I walked with a tilt to one side, like I was a hero at the end of an action movie after s/he/y's been through the shit and killed the big boss and is about to say something smart and/or snarky to h/i/r best friend or partner or precocious child s/he/y saved.

I would LOVE to say that the knot stayed gone. It isn't gone at all. In fact, it is there right now (hello old friend), but for three days, I was only everyday angry at my job instead of supersonic angry. What causes this kind of Academic Rage™? Well, it varies from place to place and person to person, but shit rolls downhill, so it is really easy to figure it out. When the boss is a malicious prick who systematically takes down rivals, be they real or perceived, or if the boss is an incompetent boob who runs roughshod over everyone Kool-Aid Man style, or if the boss chooses willful ignorance of major problems while giving speeches and shouting platitudes, or as is the case where I work, where the president has hit the trifecta, people are going to be on edge.

I got an email the other day from a colleague that read, "Morning Virgil, I was elated to see that I wasn't fired today. Hope you are well." It was meant as a joke, and I laughed, but honestly, it wasn't funny even in a "laugh or you'll cry" kind of way. It was a "laugh or I will spit venom" situation. Are there people at work that I dislike? Yes. Of course. Fucking Steve is there. Goddamn it, Steve! Give whatever it is a fucking rest already. While I feel the rage about Steve and his bullshit, I could, for the most part, find a way to get lost in my job. The actual job I was hired to do, the job I love: teaching students.

Unfortunately, right now, and at universities all across the country, there is a dearth of quality leadership. People fail up all the time. This isn't something I've made up. People who have no business being in charge end up in charge because s/he/y didn't suck at a different job. It's called the Peter Principle[16]. No, not St. Peter; he earned his job. The short version of The Peter Principle is

---

[16] Niewiesk, Stefan. "Defeating the Peter Principle in Academic Leadership." *Inside Higher Ed*, www.insidehighered.com/advice/2023/02/14/ how-avoid-peter-principle-academic-administration-opinion#.

if a man manages to sit down without sitting on his balls, he gets to be a university president. I say man here because most of my anger is directed at men. I thought time was up for white dudes, but no. #timesnotup. Fuck me. Straight. White. Dudes. Dude bro-ing their way to the top with secret handshakes and patriarchal back-slaps (never a hug because... you know... no homo). I would say my anger level is gendered 80/20 in favor of the men in charge. It is true that there are plenty of ladies who failed up and who are trash at their jobs. I've worked with several. I have yet to work for a non-binary person, but I assume some of them suck too. It happens.

The last time I raised my voice at a colleague, it was a woman who failed up so spectacularly that she didn't understand a basic concept that someone in her position should have. I was so frustrated that I snapped at her before hanging up. It was in the smartphone age, so I couldn't slam down the receiver in frustration. Not all technology is good. Being able to slam a phone down to hang up was amazing. That shit was cathartic. Where my Xers and Boomers at? You know.

Here is a snapshot of what happens. People are considered good at one thing, like say, being a history Professor. That person then is, for some reason, rewarded for being liked as a history Professor, which isn't the same thing as actually being good at it. S/he/y is just *considered* good at it. No one complains. The Professor doesn't punch a student or get stoned in the parking lot with students after class. Often s/he/y is promoted because, and this is the real kicker, s/he/y has a high "success rate," and so it is falsely assumed that person is doing a good job.

Surely, having a high success rate is a good thing. He tried not to sit on his balls and he didn't. He waited until he got home to get stoned. He tried not to punch his students and he didn't. He tried to have his students pass, and they did. All good. I want to give him a big back slap. I want to back-slap him so hard right now.

Simmer down. Keep your hands in your pants and off that straight white dude's back. Let's deconstruct that shit for a second, shall we? Not sitting on your balls isn't that hard. Just don't go commando. Christ on a stick. Getting stoned at home is just safe.

Don't toke and drive, people. Respect the human social contract. Punching students is a bit harder. Sometimes they are huge assholes because they are humans, and humans are huge assholes. Still, social contract. Power dynamic. No matter how angry a student makes you, you can always go home, take off your pants, hold onto your nuts, and get baked. All good.

The passing students thing though, that is where things get dicey. Where I currently work, as far as I know, faculty are not rated on student success rates, but in the last job I had, this was very much a thing. Essentially, if the teacher has a certain percentage of students who don't pass the course, s/he/y is "failing" at the job. It doesn't matter that the students have not mastered the material or even just become average at it.

Their learning doesn't matter. Completion rates and graduation rates matter. It is all about retention. In the past three years (hello back knot), any time I was in a meeting with an executive at my school, retention rates came up. Retention rates are based on the number of incoming students in a given cohort and how many people graduate. The numbers can be fudged, and they are all the time. If an incoming class of students is 1000 students, the goal is to get 1000 students to graduate. Of course, they won't. That isn't reasonable. Some fail. Some drop out. Some transfer. Colleges count transfers in the final numbers, so if 1000 start and only 500 of them finish, but 900 students graduate four years later, it is considered a 90 percent success rate. It is bullshit, but it is the way it is done. To get to that number, a lot of people do a lot of work with transfers and returning students and dealing with persistence (more on that below).

According to *US News and World Report*, the magazine that does this stuff the best, 1 in 3 students don't come back after year one[17]. That is pretty consistent for the overall 4-year graduation rate, which is just over 65 percent. Interestingly enough though, the persistence rate, which is based on the individual student's

---

[17] "2019 Freshman Retention Rate at National Universities | US News Rankings." *Usnews.com*, 2019, www.usnews.com/best-colleges/rankings/national-universities/freshmen-least-most-likely-return.

ability to grind it out and eventually graduate, is 75 percent[18]. Yep. 10 percent of students who graduate from a higher ed institution finish outside of the 4-year window, likely at a different institution from where they started. So, 25 percent of students start college and don't finish. Again, the reasons vary, but a lot of them are personal and not intellectual. 75 percent of them are successful. Let's party.

This number seems good to me. I am not a person who thinks the team should win the championship every year. If my favorite team's coach manages to win 75 percent of the time, s/he/y can be coach for life. It isn't realistic to think that every coach can be Pat Summitt and clock a nearly 92% win percentage[19]. There is a reason there is a statue of her on the University of Tennessee's campus. She was a queen. While I do struggle with the fact that at major colleges, the coaches are often the highest-paid employees, I do think there is a reasonable analogy to be made here.

Winning percentages matter. If a salesperson lands a sale 51 percent of the time s/he/y makes a call, that should, in my estimation, make that person a success. I knew nothing about sales, so I did some research, and I discovered that in the sales world, a 20 percent close rate is average, and thus, that must mean it is good. 20 percent close rate[20]. Holy shit. That is lower than baseball. I mean, if a guy has a 300-hitting percentage, he will make millions of dollars failing 70 percent of the time. I know there is more to it, but people who suck at defense play right field or are designated hitters, and they make millions.

So seriously, 65 percent should be time to party; that is a huge number. Alas, no one is partying. 65 percent isn't good enough. There is a greed factor here, and there will be a whole chapter on

---

[18] "Student Persistence vs. Retention in Higher Education." *Moderncampus. com*, moderncampus.com/blog/persistence-vs-retention.html.

[19] "Pat Summitt - Women's Basketball Coach." *University of Tennessee Athletics*, utsports.com/sports/womens-basketball/roster/coaches/ pat-summitt/608.

[20] Coleman, Basha. "Sales Close Rate Industry Benchmarks: How Does Your Close Rate Compare?" *Blog.hubspot.com*, blog.hubspot.com/sales/new-sales-close-rate-industry-benchmarks-how-does-your-close-rate-compare.

greed later, so don't worry, but that is why this number isn't good enough. The people in charge are not being realistic. 65 percent is a high success rate. If 20 percent is a good rate for sales and 30 percent is a good rate for hitters, and Americans will elect a president who loses the popular vote, 65 percent should be a HUGE win.

Still, it isn't because of ego. Because it "looks bad." We are fucking educators. We need to educate people that the retention rate is good enough and that the persistence rate, the 75 percent number, is what we, the collective WE of higher ed, should be proud of. I am fucking proud of it. Still no dice. More graduates mean more press, which means more money, which means I have a bigger penis.

The higher the retention rate, the more successful a school or a person is. So, back to the point of this whole diversion: individual success rates. If the aforementioned history Professor has a 95-100 percent success rate, he is doing a great job, which gets him a promotion to Chair, then Dean, then VP, and then, in my case, President of the university. He has been rewarded all along for getting super high retention rates.

Super high retention rates keep students, and students bring in money, be it their own or federal loans. The measure of success for a teacher is learning. Most teachers would prefer not to give out grades. We want students to learn. The problem is that learning doesn't pay the bills; graduation rates do. Retention is all that matters, and so, all those years ago when the history Professor had that amazing completion rate, he was likely doing it on the back of grade inflation.

Grade inflation is just what it sounds like. It is giving students a grade they didn't earn to make sure they pass the class. If you want to be sure you have a 95 percent success rate in your class or a 95 percent retention rate, what do you do? You make the students happy. You inflate the services on campus by giving them all a gym membership or cookies and ice cream in the cafeteria, or you build a lazy river through campus, and of course, you make sure they all pass even if they didn't learn anything. If you can get your school's retention rate into the 90s, you become a rock star. If you make that promise, and based on your past performances of "success," you will be an amazing leader. Fail. Right. The. Fuck. Up.

Learning isn't the measure of success anymore[21].

Let that hang for a second.

If customers suddenly stopped shopping at Target, it would go under. It seems unlikely. Target is pretty awesome, but it happens. Remember Radio Shack? Remember Circuit City? Remember Sears? They all seemed indestructible, and yet, they went down because they didn't focus on the customer experience and do what the customers wanted. Learning isn't the measure of success any longer because the idiots in charge of higher education are trying to learn lessons from those seemingly too big-to-fail companies. Retention is the most important thing because higher education is now and shall forever be a business.

Hamlet said in Act III Scene I, "It hath made me mad."[22] Scholars argue if he means "angry" or "crazy." I would argue, that shit like this, this failing up, this treating college like business, this idea that executives get bonuses[23] for graduation rates instead of job placements or entry into grad schools, this idea that we call the college leaders executives in the first place as though education is a commodity that means nothing and has no value except for keeping one's job, instead of a reward for hard work and persistence, hath made me fucking mad.

[21] Hanlon, Aaron R. "I Know Why College Grades Are Going Up. It's Definitely Not Wokeism." *The New Republic*, newrepublic.com/article/178657/grade-inflation-college-not-wokeism. Accessed 8 June 2024.

[22] Shakespeare, William. "Hamlet - Act 3, Scene 1 | Folger Shakespeare Library." *Www.folger.edu*, www.folger.edu/explore/shakespeares-works/hamlet/read/3/1/.

[23] Wilde, James Finkelstein, Judith. "Bonuses and Benefits." *Inside Higher Ed*, www.insidehighered.com/advice/2017/05/25/examination-growing-number-perks-and-bonuses-college-presidents-essay.

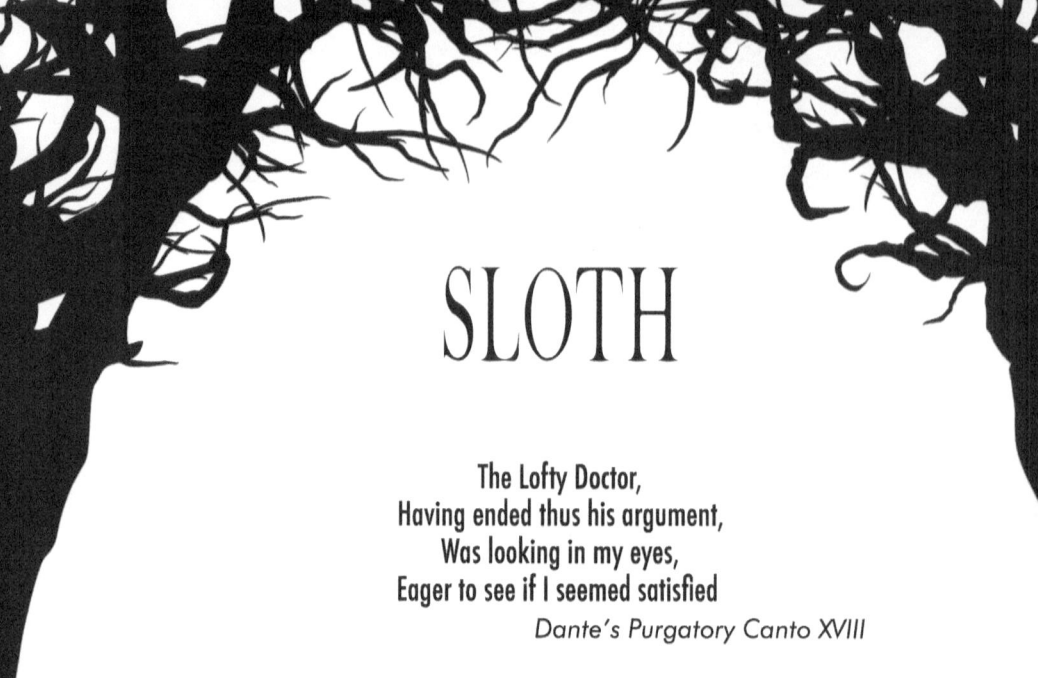

SLOTH

The Lofty Doctor,
Having ended thus his argument,
Was looking in my eyes,
Eager to see if I seemed satisfied

Dante's Purgatory Canto XVIII

THERE ARE TWO KINDS OF TEACHERS IN THE

world. I know, I know; it isn't good to be so binary. We don't live in that kind of world anymore, and that is a good thing. I am all for it. There should be more choices than just two. We should have open primaries. We should eliminate political parties. Pronouns are problematic. I understand. I agree. Still, there are two kinds of teachers. There are those who are visionary and those who want to hold down a chair. The visionaries are the ones who abhor sloth, and obviously, those who want to hold down a chair have made complacency an art form.

They are the slothiest of the slothy. They are so comfortable they are almost bored. They only get fired up when someone asks them to move just a little. They've spent years getting this office space just right. The chair is the right amount of broken in. They have the perfect teaching schedule that they've done exactly the same for the past 30 years. If they can just stay put for another 10-30 years, they can retire with Emeritus status (college for "you get to keep your office and/or library card and people still have to call you Professor even though you don't do that job anymore"), or better yet, they can die right there in that chair and become the stuff of legend.

Inside each of those categories are various degrees. Not everyone is a visionary who can see the future, but they don't impede change. In the hold-down-a-chair types, some are willing to maybe get a standing desk. Those two people are standing near the center of the spectrum. They are unwilling to cause a lot of drama. A standing desk person and a don't impede change person could share an office and agree on 99 percent of the things like being annoyed at having to share an office.

Like anything, it is a spectrum. There are certainly those visionaries who want to change things for the sake of change. They are agents of chaos who react out of fear or who chase trends. They are, let's say, at the far left of the spectrum. If we use the political spectrum as an example, they are so far to the left that they are borderline anarchists. They've started wanting universal health care and ended up demanding everyone pay 95 percent of their paycheck to the federal government. These folks don't speak for the rest of the visionary crowd, but they make so much noise that everyone ends up listening. I mean, Antifa stands for "Anti-Fascist." That must be a good thing. Maybe dressing like fascists and acting like a bunch of fuckheads who dox people and throw shit through the windows of a small business whose owner is just trying to sell overpriced t-shits to tourists sort of undercuts the point. Maybe. I'm just saying.

Oftentimes, when people get so far to the extreme on either end of the spectrum, they bend it around and end up saying some of the points of the other "side." Think Libertarians. Yes. I want rights for everyone, and I want my privacy, but maybe I want libraries, open education, and roads to be free. We will spend some time on that end of the academic spectrum in the next two chapters, so we don't need to worry. While the lazyasses are about to take some verbal punches to the nose, the chaos agents will have their time in the barrel.

On the other end of the spectrum, or all the way around the back in this analogy, are those who are holding down a chair so hard that they refuse to let anything go for any reason. Generally, but not always, those people are Full Professors. They feel as though they are the only people who can do the job that they do, and they think that there is only one way to do the job. They cast aspersions and plant false flags because they think higher education has been working fine for thousands of years, so there is no need to make any changes.

This often means they resist transfer credits from other schools or courses being taught in other modalities. I've heard people say that online courses are bad. I mentioned this in the last chapter, but it is worth repeating here. Of course, some online courses are bad, because some of them are, but not all online courses are bad. A well-designed, asynchronous online course is highly effective and offers many benefits not available in an on-ground course or a synchronous online course[24].

Spoiler alert: some courses are bad regardless of modality. Often, the reason is some old, cranky, lazyass fuck holding down a chair is using the same book he used when he started teaching this course in the last century (It is not always a he, but it often is, fucking Steve). Thus, they assume that anyone with new ideas is taking a sledgehammer to the foundation of higher education.

There are so many issues with these people, but we shall focus on just a few of their arguments. I'm not here to nitpick. I am not an extremist, even though higher education is full of them. I know that sometimes these people have valid points. Sometimes, we need to replace that one janky cart that pulls hard to the left. I get it. I agree. We don't ban all shopping carts just because one is bad. There is a lot of all-or-nothing bravado. You say bravado; I say bullshit.

Let's look at the idea that these people are the only ones who can do the job they were hired to do. There are so many problems with this, and yet, the Slotherstons (That is their surname from now on) are willing to use this obvious fabrication to justify why no one else should be brought in and why they shouldn't be asked to change. The obvious fallacy in this argument is that these people were taught by someone else and likely not at the institution where they are currently teaching. Considering that 20 percent of the

---

24 MIT Open Learning. "The 5 Benefits of Asynchronous Learning." *Curve. mit.edu*, 15 Dec. 2021, curve.mit.edu/5-benefits-asynchronous-learning.

programs that grant PhDs are responsible for 80 percent[25] of the full-time faculty across the country, the math doesn't work. We will revisit those numbers in the next book, so don't worry. I don't want you to think I am glossing over that shocking bit of news. Talk about an academic circle jerk. In this argument, it means that the vast majority of people teach at institutions other than the school they attended.

So, that means these people are trying to claim that only they can teach a certain program, but they learned the information from someone else somewhere else. Let me use a highly educated turn of phrase here to respond: No fucking shit. Duh. I learned from my Professors, some of whom went to those elite 20 percent circle-jerk schools, but many went to other places. The best poetry teacher I had went to a state school that most people outside of the state, and I would guess half of the people inside the state, didn't even know existed. He had a contract with one of the major academic publishers to translate poetry from several European languages, and there he was, teaching me.

I learned from him, and when I teach poetry, I pay it forward. I am part of his teaching lineage, but it doesn't mean that I am the ONLY person who can teach poetry. I have been successful teaching poetry, and I have struck out regardless of if I taught it on-ground or online or as a hybrid (not Hi-Bird as many people say. People with whom I work. Many who have degrees from the circle-jerk schools see the word hybrid and say Hi-Bird. They teach English. Fuck me). If I teach it in any modality, I have my way to teach it, and that way may or may not reach the student. There is a real give-and-take in the educational relationship, and so, I am not the only person at my college who can teach poetry. I shouldn't be the only person. If you are going to college, and there is only one person who teaches all the courses in one subject, something is wrong. I can think of five other people who are qualified to do it and do it well, and one qualified person who should stop. She sucks.

---

[25] Flaherty, Colleen. "Prestige Hiring across Academe." *Inside Higher Ed*, www.insidehighered.com/news/2022/09/23/ new-study-finds-80-faculty-trained-20-institutions.

I recently had a robust disagreement with someone who said math could not be taught online. Not that this person couldn't or didn't want to, but that "it" couldn't be done. Really? Hmmm. One quick search of online math courses shows that there are literally hundreds of fully accredited, high-level schools, some of them in the circle-jerk group (This person didn't go to one of those schools so…), are teaching math online right now. Those thieving bastards. How dare they? We should demand they give all those students their money back. SCAM!!!

Of course, what this person was saying was that *he* couldn't do it well, his students didn't find his online course effective, and that he didn't like it. All of those things are fair. He doesn't have to like it. He doesn't HAVE to do it, but it doesn't mean he should get in the way of other people doing it. That is what a Normalton would say, but a Slotherton knows that if anyone moves in this direction, and they are effective and the students like it, then they might HAVE to do it as well. This isn't change for the sake of change. This is change the students want. Not because they are lazy. Online courses take a lot more work than sitting passively in an on-ground course. They like these options because they are fucking busy. Around 60 percent of the students participate in an extracurricular activity[26]. So yeah, maybe taking math online frees them up to save the bees or whatever it is they are saving, attend a protest, go to softball practice, or work to save up to take the math class, or whatever it is they are doing.

See, the thing about the Slothertons is that they hang on to the way things used to be because the way things used to be really, really benefits them. Sure, for years and years, centuries and centuries, education was old-white guys forcing young white guys to repeat things over and over until they memorized those things, and then they took tests that showed they memorized the "facts," and they were then considered educated. While memorization is something that works for many subjects, it doesn't have anything to do with learning. Students have, for centuries and centuries,

---

[26] Linder, Jannik. "College Students Involved in Extracurricular Activities Statistics [Fresh Research] • Gitnux." *Gitnux.org*, gitnux.org/college-students-involved-in-extracurricular-activities-statistics/.

known this instinctively and asked the question, "When am I ever going to use this in real life?" I had an amazing math teacher tell me the answer because I was certainly an asshole as a student. Yep. Math. Wow. It is so much more valuable than just adding (Although we will do some sexy, sexy math in the next chapter, so it is still good in its purest form).

The answer is that you may not use calculus in "real life," but you will use the problem-solving skills you learned to, oh, I don't know, solve a problem. You might use your ability to analyze why a battle during WWI failed to use the cause and effect relationships to figure out how to stop a bad procedure from taking hold at your company. Although, this is not likely because for whatever reason Americans have a hard-on for WWII, and we hardly ever learn anything about WWI. Something about an Archduke and his wife in Serbia? Where the fuck is Serbia? What is an Archduke? Is that from *Bridgerton*?

In 1983, Howard Gardner[27] really pissed the Slothertons off when he threw out this idea that there was more than one way to learn, and that different people learn differently. It was almost like he slapped the Slothertons across the face and challenged them to a duel. He made the case that rote memorization isn't the only way people can learn things. He didn't say one CAN'T learn that way, but that it isn't the only way. This meant that if this were true, then teachers would have to come up with different ways to reach everyone. Maybe, just maybe, the fidgety kid in the back row might do better if s/he/y had the chance to get up and touch something or move around while learning instead of being in the back row with h/i/r feet on the ground and h/i/r back ramrod straight. Yeah, but if that is true, then that sounds like a lot of work. Teachers might have to do something different. It has worked for thousands of years; everything is fine. There was a bit of a revolution, but the Slothertons never really let it go. In fact, in recent years, there has been a lot of research done to disprove Gardner's

---

[27] Edutopia. "Multiple Intelligences: What Does the Research Say?" *Edutopia*, George Lucas Educational Foundation, 20 July 2016, www.edutopia.org/multiple-intelligences-research.

theory's effectiveness[28]. No one disputes that people learn differently, but there is an argument that knowing how we learn changes how much information we can take in and process.

Look, I am not here to praise or shit on Gardner. Like any educational theory, I like some of it and think some of it needs more research. Theories are like that. They are not perfect. They advance ideas, and we build upon them. Still, I find it profoundly disturbing that the Slothertons spend so much time and energy trying to disprove something instead of trying to find a way to include the best parts of Gardner's findings in their teaching style.

Slothertons are like scam artists in that way. Imagine if people spent just a fraction of the time they spent running a scam on doing something productive; not only would they not be criminals, but they would likely be quite successful. I have told multiple students on multiple occasions that if they spent as much time on the assignment as they did complaining about the grade, they would have done exponentially better on the assignment. No, you can't have "extra credit" when you didn't do the "regular credit." If you couldn't do the assignment correctly in the month that you had it, why would you be able to do the extra work in the final 48 hours before final grades are due?

Lazy students and lazy teachers are so similar. Seriously, there is a whole other book of anecdotes I could write about teachers doing the same thing they complained about 10 seconds after they complained. It is the most bizarre form of dissociation I've ever seen. Like, can you hear the words you are saying? I know I can.

These lazy fucks don't want to try. They don't want to change. They don't want to do anything new. They lie and make bullshit claims and appeal to antiquity because the alternative involves work. They would rather spend a few years trying to tear down someone else's ideas that involve change or advancement than use that time to get better. Why? Because getting better involves trying. It involves caring about students and not a 3-month summer vacation and a sweet office and the godlike power that comes with holding someone hostage twice a week for 90 minutes

---

[28] Chick, Nancy. "Learning Styles." *Vanderbilt University*, 10 June 2010, cft. vanderbilt.edu/guides-sub-pages/learning-styles-preferences/.

while droning on and on saying the same, boring, tired lecture and giving the same, boring, tired test from the same boring tired textbooks. Also, this chair is incredibly comfortable.

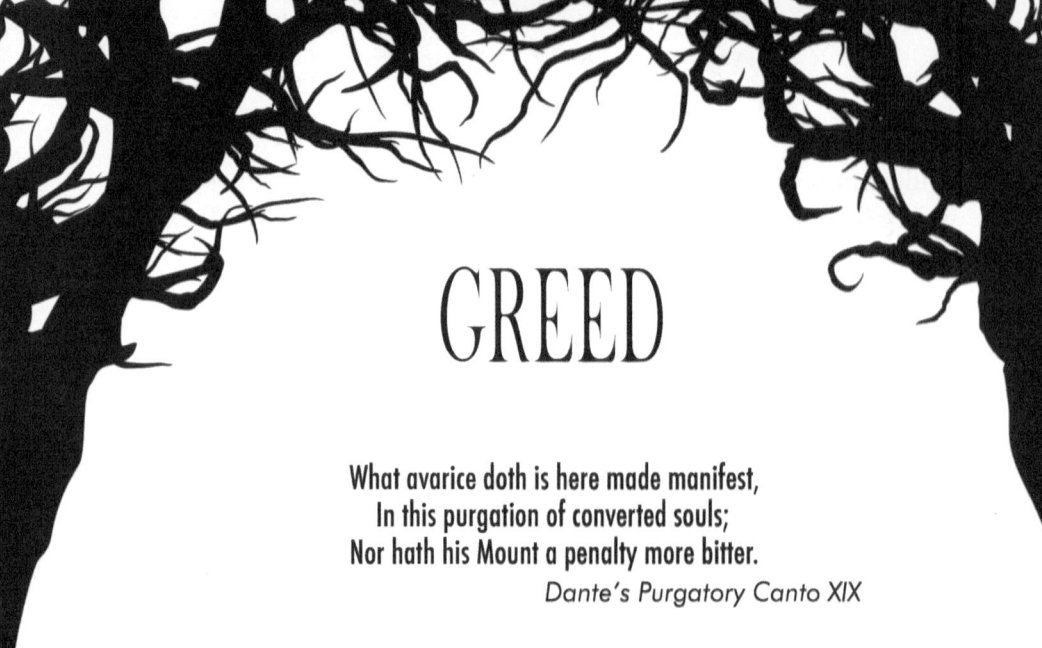

GREED

What avarice doth is here made manifest,
In this purgation of converted souls;
Nor hath his Mount a penalty more bitter.

Dante's Purgatory Canto XIX

GORDON GEKKO WAS THE VILLAIN IN THE MOVIE

Wall Street[29]. Like, it isn't up for debate. He is a bad, bad guy. Statistically speaking, most people have not seen this movie, so it would be good for me to explain a few things. The plot revolves around an up-and-coming stockbroker called Bud Fox. Yeah. Not subtle. He is a dude who is being hunted and is also clever. Wow. Anyway, Bud wants to be in with Gekko, who is like the Eric Clapton of Wall Street, and make a shit ton of cash. Desperate to get hired, he does some inside trading, gets rich, and thinks he is going to be set forever. Gekko gives the big greed speech, and people cream their jeans. Michael Douglas won an Oscar for it, and that speech is replayed all the time.

Before there was even a term for it, there was some strange Mandela Effect with it. For some reason, people think the movie is advocating greed and think Gekko is a hero. There is a very "live fast, die young, and leave a-good-looking corpse" vibe happening there. In his heyday, I would have cast Gekko as James Dean, so I get that part, but the problem is that wasn't the point of the film. Oliver Stone wasn't saying greed is good. He was saying that greed is bad. Look at this guy. He is a monster. The point was missed, unfortunately.

---

[29] *Wall Street.* Directed by Oliver Stone. 1987. 20th Century Fox.

One could argue, and I am one and I am thus arguing, that Patrick Bateman from *American Psycho*[30] is commenting on the Gekko lovers. That book and subsequent movie feature a sociopath who is so bad that the book and film title call him a psycho. Couldn't be clearer, right? Bateman commits every crime imaginable and gets away with it because he is a rich white guy who is part of the capitalistic system. Easton Ellis is trying to show readers what could happen if capitalism runs amok. Unfortunately, people read that book or saw the film version and got the wrong idea about that character as well. In both cases, the wrong people, mostly straight white dudes, think that those guys are heroes. They are not. Stop. Seriously. Get a fucking grip.

These are the same idiots who later went on to co-op the red pill idea from *The Matrix*[31]. That film is a trans allegory. This is not up for debate. The writers and directors were assigned male at birth and are trans women. They are women. When Neo takes the red pill and wakes up from the matrix, that was them saying that we were trapped in a simulation where we were born men, but in the real world, we are women. In the film, these women have a Hawaiian guy doing kung-fu, and they cast Carrie Anne Moss as a badass. Laurence Fishburn is named after a god. The white dudes in this movie are not great. Joey Pants is super white. He is a white, white guy, and he plays a villain in the film. He turns on the good guys. The other baddie, Agent Smith, is played by Hugo Weaving, and he is so white that he goes on to play the Red Skull in the Marvel movies. The woman and the non-white characters are the clear heroes in the film that was created by two women and yet... sigh.

Unfortunately, the red-pillers[32] of now use this term to mean they are "awake" from the world where trans people have rights,

---

[30] Bret Easton Ellis. *American Psycho*. New York, Vintage Contemporaries / Random House, 1991.

[31] *The Matrix*. Directed by The Wachowskis. 1999. Warner Brothers.

[32] Marche, Stephen. "Swallowing the Red Pill: A Journey to the Heart of Modern Misogyny." *The Guardian*, 14 Apr. 2016, www.theguardian.com/technology/2016/apr/14/ the-red-pill-reddit-modern-misogyny-manosphere-men.

women have rights, and so they, the white men, are being harmed in some way. Giving rights to someone has never, ever taken rights away from someone else. There isn't a limit on the amount of rights folks can have. Rights are limitless. Yet the red-pillers think Gekko and Bateman are heroes. They think Neo is a white guy because they really, really want him to be. They are fucking idiots. They are a problem. A big, white, douchey problem.

I work for a lot of straight white guys. Higher ed has a shit-ton of them. Interestingly enough, the majority of non-tenure-track, adjunct, and at-will employees are women, but 56 percent of tenure-track jobs go to men and 64 percent of Full Professorships go to men.[33] In contrast, 77 percent of K-12 teachers are women[34]. K-12 teachers do more work for longer and for less pay. Yeah. So there is that. Shit is all fucked up everywhere. This isn't that book, but we could do that maybe as a follow-up when this series is done (wink).

Notice I used the word "for" up there and not "with." That was intentional. Only 30 percent of college presidents are women, and only 5 percent of them are women of color. Some people in this job are called Chancellor, which is well, I don't want to offend my German readers, but that word has connotations, right? Colleges are generally overseen by a board of directors who are the group ultimately responsible for the hiring or firing of the presidents. 70 percent of college board members have a penis (or present as male, but let's be honest, the college boards are not trans people). Sometimes it is between their legs, but often it is in place of their heads, and so, they hire other people with dicks and/or who are dicks to run the shows, and they back slap and bro hug and all that shit. Blech.

Anyway, those mostly white, mostly male douchey douches got the wrong idea about Gordon, Patrick, and likely several other white rich assholes from pop culture or their lives or both, and so they think that being rich, making money, having status, living in

[33] "Fast Facts: Women Working in Academia." *AAUW : Empowering Women since 1881*, www.aauw.org/resources/article/fast-facts-academia/.

[34] National Center for Education Statistics. "COE - Characteristics of Public School Teachers." *Nces.ed.gov*, May 2021, nces.ed.gov/programs/coe/indicator/clr/public-school-teachers.

a free home, which is often palatial, which is a real thing on many campuses[35], is something they deserve just because they are white guys. The house thing, by the way, is real. It is absurd, and of course, the college I attended had one. The president added a pool while I was there. It is warm like seven days a year where I went to college, so... white guy needs an outdoor pool.

The houses are often named for past presidents, which ultimately is the goal for all these dudes. They want to have their names on something. The business card scene in *American Psycho* says it all. There is a scene that goes on for quite a while where these rich asshats debate what shade of, wait for it, *white* their cards are. It is so, so funny and disturbing how much they give a shit about the shade of white their business card is. This is nothing other than brilliant satire. Yet now, decades later, shit like this shows up in real life, and people forget it wasn't supposed to be a good thing.

Start with your name on a card, end with your name on a building, or have a scholarship or foundation named after you, and you can live forever! Amazing. The real important thing in your legacy shouldn't be how many students you educated or how many of them went on to affect society in a positive way. The real way you know you've made it is when someone takes a shit in an unwashed bathroom during halftime of a game in the gym with your name on it. Success!

Thus, we can imagine what happens when rich white douchey assholes get in charge of things: they think about making money and the free market and all that stuff. They start thinking about what programs make money and what programs lose money. They start thinking about what other rich white douches say about the "value" of education, and things sort of lose perspective in a hurry. Of course, don't point out they live in a free house while working for a non-profit (Yes, of course, there are for-profit schools. They are not all scams, just most of them are, and that is a whole other book). They "earned" that, and it is part of their "wages," but I'll

---

[35] *Official Residences of Presidents and Chancellors of Universities and Colleges - Karen Kaler*. 25 Mar. 2023, www.karen-kaler.com/blog/official-residences-of-presidents-and-chancellors-of-universities-and-colleges/.

bet you a bag of donuts they don't claim that shit on their taxes. You say tomato; I say tax evasion.

The problem with all of this is that the concept of "enough" doesn't exist. This is the problem with unregulated capitalism. I'm not breaking any new ground here; this is all just reality. To these people, breaking even isn't acceptable, even though the point of a non-profit is to break even. I understand that non-profits shouldn't lose money either, and unless the company is run by Mackenzie Scott[36], losing money isn't the plan. Still, I was recently at a meeting with the "executives" at my university, and one of them suggested that we play AC/DC's "Back in Black" when the president walked in because we were set to make money. While s/he/y high-fived and hero-worshiped the straight white dude and fantasized about how hard s/he/y was going to slap that sweet sweaty back of his while s/he/y danced and shook h/i/r money maker, I puked in my mouth a little. Okay. I puked in it a lot.

Why? Why would my university making money make me sick? Well, so many reasons. The main reason though is that instead of investing the money and fixing up a broken building or hiring more full-time faculty, many of these non-profit schools keep their non-profit status by giving existing full-time people bonuses. Yep. The size of the bonus depends on the position, but rest assured, the money doesn't trickle down to the right people. Instead of investing and growing or paying adjuncts a better wage or making the insurance more affordable or holding tuition rates down or making books free for students, the people at the top get a bonus. The further one is down the ladder, the smaller the bonus. I know because I worked at one of these places for a time.

It may be hypocritical of me to accept the money because for three of the eleven years I worked there, I received a bonus. I justify it still today because I was not a full-time employee. I worked full-time hours and had a year-by-year contract, and I was required to teach 12 courses per year, (Most full-time faculty teach 8 per year) and I had to attend faculty meetings and do administrative work,

---

[36] Liu, Phoebe. "MacKenzie Scott Has Donated $2.2 Billion to Charity This Year." *Forbes*, www.forbes.com/sites/phoebeliu/2023/12/08/mackenzie-scott-has-donated-22-billion-to-charity-this-year/?sh=a4f3130c1439.

but I wasn't given any health benefits. So, I took the money. It was a few hundred dollars. One of the three years, I took a nice vacation. The rest of the time, I spent that money on bills. One time, I used it to have dental work done. Also, because I wasn't a college president, and the bonus wasn't a free home or car or both, I was taxed on the money. Bonus! YAY!

I just see things differently. I don't think our job in non-profit higher education is to make money to line our pockets. If our college makes money, we need to invest. We know that we have an adjunct problem as I detailed in the last book. We know there is always something else the school could use: more books in the library or another tutor in the math lab or an actual math lab or writing lab or whatever lab. I can promise every school could use another Title IX coordinator (My school has one), another mental health counselor (My school has one), or an administrative assistant (My college has three). All of those things would be a great use of money. Having the president walking in blaring AC/DC isn't the right message.

Our job in higher ed isn't supposed to be to have more money. We don't want to hoard cash. We want to hoard knowledge. Our goal is to have more knowledge and learn as much as possible, but even then, we need to temper that a bit by diversifying what we learn. The focus of education isn't to just learn one thing. It is to learn a lot of things. Sure, a degree in, say, marketing, prepares one to be a professional marketer. That is great. However, as a well-educated person, a marketing major taking something like an art appreciation class might allow h/i/r to have a different approach to a project that could ultimately land h/i/r the job.

While it is true that I think one can never have enough knowledge or one can never spend enough time reading books, listening to music, or making and consuming art, some things are limitless, but even they should be controlled. You don't want to ONLY listen to one song from your favorite band over and over. You don't want to ONLY read one book over and over. Knowledge is limitless, but, like those breadsticks at Olive Garden, you eventually need to stop, or you will fill up before the other stuff comes. Read your favorite book once a year. Listen to your favorite song every day. The rest of the time, you should expand your knowledge base and grow, not for the sake of growing, but in a way that makes sense to you where there is a benefit not only to you but to the people in your life.

Presidents and the other "executive" people in the C-suite[37], which believe it or not is yet another business term that is used in higher ed, gorge on that bread and still shove the full unlimited pasta into their mouths. These are the people in power, and they set the tone, but they are out of step with the rest of the people in higher ed. Most people in higher ed are the students because they outnumber everyone. According to data, the national average of students to faculty is 18:1[38]. Each college has its own makeup of C-Suite executives, but most of the ones I've worked for have between 8-12 "voting" members. That number doesn't change. If the school has 1000 students, that would mean 10 executives and 55 faculty members. If there are 20,000 students, that would mean around 1,100 members of faculty while there would still be only 10 executives.

The more students and faculty a college has, the more money the executives make, the bigger house they have, and the more trips they get to take to raise money for the school. Oh yeah, did I fail to mention that? The main job of most college presidents is to raise money. In 2023, 58 Billion[39] (with a capital B) dollars were donated to colleges and universities, but almost none of that goes to personnel. No one wants to give 1 million dollars to pay someone to teach. Keep in mind that money could, in theory, fund a full-time faculty member's salary for around 15 years. My former president said that people will give money for a scholarship or a building but never for salaries. Why? You can't name a faculty member after yourself, but you can take a shit on one.

---

[37] Bloomenthal, Andrew. "Seeing the C-Suite." *Investopedia*, 2019, www.investopedia.com/terms/c/c-suite.asp.

[38] "35 Best College Student-Faculty Ratios for 2024." *Colleges of Distinction,* collegesofdistinction.com/advice/35-best-student-faculty-college-ratios/.

[39] "US Colleges Received $58B in Philanthropic Support in FY23." *Higher Ed Dive,* www.highereddive.com/news/us-college-giving-donations-case/708165/.

GLUTTONY

The love of taste stirs
Not too great a longing in their breast,
But always hunger only
Dante's Purgatory Canto XXIV

HIGHER EDUCATION DOESN'T SEEM LIKE A PLACE for gluttons. Well, gluttons for punishment for sure. I have no research on this, and I don't want to sully up my search engine algorithm by searching, but I wouldn't be shocked to learn that a lot of folks in higher ed are part of the BDSM community. Pain as pleasure and all of that. Generally, when one thinks of higher ed, people don't imagine a person who gorges on sweets until one bursts like that scene in *The Meaning of Life*[40] where the guy eats and eats until he bursts on his mint at the end of the meal. Gross.

That isn't to say that being in higher ed doesn't take a toll on one's body. In my 30 years as a higher educator, I've weighed as little as 170 pounds and as much as 260 pounds. While a lot of those weight fluctuations had to do with stress eating or stress eating away at me, some of it had to do with being healthy while regulating my food intake through the use of portion control, daily exercise, and therapy. I certainly appeared "typically" gluttonous when I was at my peak weight.

Of course, being gluttonous has very little to do with physical attributes. As we saw in the previous chapter, some people are super greedy, and that comes from being drunk with power. About half of the students in higher ed meet the criteria for having

---

[40] *The Meaning of Life*. Directed by Terry Jones. 1983. The Monty Python Partnership. Universal Pictures.

a substance abuse disorder.[41] So, you know, that is incredibly problematic, but because it is disguised as "partying" and not a cry for help, nothing is done. That is typical behavior for "kids" these days because it was what we did back "in my day." If it is gluttonous and destructive behavior that gets passed down from generation to generation, it is a "tradition," but if these blasted kids spend too much time on TikTok, we better ban that. Back in my day, we didn't have TikTok; we got our voyeurism the old-fashioned way with binoculars and a ladder.

While all of this is real and gross and we should spend some time looking into all of that, we are going to take a look at the full-time faculty who are stuck here on this terrace of Purgatory. Like those "kids" who are legally adults who can vote, smoke, and serve in the military, who have perpetuated ritualistic behavior by binge drinking, hoarding drugs, or hazing (or all three), the faculty perpetuate ritualistic behavior by bingeing on power and accolades, hoarding classes, or hazing (or all three). We will spend a bit more time on hazing in the next chapter, as that isn't so much gluttonous but just shitty, and the people who do it are shitty. While it doesn't seem to have much to do with Lust, I will make an argument. I may fail. I fail all the time, although if you are still reading this book at this stage of the game, you either think I didn't fail, or it is a hate read. Either way. Thanks.

I work with a person who recently said in a meeting, "I don't really want to be the department chair, but if I only do it for one year, it looks bad, so I will do it for another year. It will look good on my CV." A CV, for those not in the know, is higher ed speak for a resume. It has all the same information that is on a resume, but unlike a resume, which is supposed to be 1-2 pages max and have relevant information for the job in question, a CV can be as long as the person wishes it to be. It is presented in reverse chronological order, beginning with what one is currently doing and ending when the person's parents loved each other very much and shared a special hug.

[41] Mosel, Stacy. "Guide to Substance Abuse and Mental Health in College." *American Addiction Centers*, 2023, americanaddictioncenters.org/rehab-guide/college.

Before we get into this statement, I feel it is important to point out that this person didn't say this randomly after a few too many pints at the bar after a long day. This person said this in a division meeting. What is the difference between a division and a department? Great question. Well, the long answer is that it depends. Some colleges will break up divisions by the traditional "schools." Some places even call them schools of... something. So there might be a school or division of science or business or social science. Inside each of those things are departments. In the business division, there could be marketing, accounting, and management. The people in that group meet as a group, and then they meet in smaller groups.

Sports do this all the time. American football has the most one-way players, that is, people who only do one thing, and thus it has the most need for splitting people up and then splitting them up again. There is a head coach, then coordinators for offense, defense, and special teams. For those not in the know, that is the kicking stuff. Most of American football is played with hands, but handball is a different game. That is like racquetball without the racquet. I suppose that makes it like squash without the racquet as well. Although there is another version of handball that is like lacrosse without the sticks. Good lord.

Anyway, the offense has a coach for each position or group of positions. The quarterbacks, linemen, running backs, and receivers all have their coaches. Each of those coaches reports to the coordinator who reports to the head coach. During the games, the coordinators make the play calls based on the information they get from the position coaches. They decide who is going to play which positions at which times. However, at any time during the game, the head coach can jump in and override the play call or personnel choices and do something different. Sometimes, the tight ends have coaches separate from the receiver coaches. Sounds exhausting and a bit bloated? Maybe even a bit gluttonous? That is what higher ed is like.

The Humanities division, of which I am a part, has departments for English, philosophy, religion, history, liberal arts studies, and communications. In some schools, history is located in social science alongside psychology, sociology, anthropology, social work, and things like that, and in other schools, liberal arts studies *is* the name for the humanities division. At my school, nursing is not part of the science division because it is its own thing with physical therapy under that. Sound like arbitrary bullshit? It is.

Thus, the head of each department reports to the head of the division who reports to the dean, who reports to the provost, who reports to the president. In the American football scenario, the department chair is the tight ends' coach. It doesn't have a ton of glamor inside the organization, but to the outside world, it sounds amazing. If I were the tight ends' coach for the New York Jets, I could parlay that into a low six-figure job as a sports anchor in a mid-sized TV market because it would seem as though I had a lot of credibility about all sports, but really, I only knew one thing well.

Going back to the statement this person made: "I don't really want to be the department chair, but if I only do it for one year, it looks bad, so I will do it for another year. It will look good on my CV." This person said this in a division meeting with the division chair present. If we run this through the higher ed to normal speak translator, the department chair said to her boss, "I have had a terrible time doing this job thus far. I am not very good at it, but I am going to hold down this chair and do very little so it looks like I did a lot because I am actively seeking other employment elsewhere."

While the job is often thankless and full of a lot of work for which one isn't paid very well, being the chair of the department is a place where one can institute some really good changes. The department chair can rewrite the curriculum to meet the students where they are. S/he/y can update the outcomes so that the courses are relevant. S/he/y can eliminate some redundant classes or create new and innovative ones. There are some small rewards there. Since, in theory, we all got into this job to serve others, those small rewards should be enough. I am currently the chair of several departments, and I spend my time doing all of the above. I am proud of the work I do. I do it for the pride, not for the accolades, and certainly not for the money.

The difference between me and this other person is that she puts her title, her rank, and links to all of her publishing history in her email signature. She has a link to her personal website, so people can, if they wish, buy copies of her books. I simply sign mine "Virgil." Shockingly, I don't have links to these books there. She doesn't really care about the work, but she is hoarding the titles so they make her look good. Gluttony at its finest.

With the power of being department chair comes the power of the schedule. Doing the schedule can be a bit of a headache, and it never feels settled until five minutes before the semester starts, but I find it fun. It is like doing a word puzzle. When I sit down to do the schedule, the first thing I do is make sure the full-time faculty have the right number of classes. I set it up so that their classes fill first. I put them in classes that I know will have the most students. I do this for myself as well. If my class has 10 students and the adjuncts have 30, I will move 20 students into my class. I am being paid triple what adjuncts are, so I should do triple the work. More students mean more assignments to grade, more conferences to have, and more feedback to give. More is more, and since I am being paid more, it only seems fair.

Other people don't do this. They hoard the low-enrolled classes for themselves. They will manipulate the schedule to ensure they are doing the least amount of work for the maximum pay. It is gross and wrong and intentional. I know it is intentional because I intentionally do the opposite. This isn't a situation where we are trying to prove a negative or base a decision on a hypothetical. I know I am doing the right thing, and it is pretty easy to do because of math. Let me give you an example using some old-timey, unsexy math. Sure, there is always fuzzy math that is manipulated to make something look better or worse than it is, but for the sake of this example, we are going to use actual math. The math you learn in your math class. Math: Balancing the books before Archimedes[42].

As I explained in the previous book, seven students are considered the break-even number at most small colleges, but if an adjunct is teaching the course, it is lower. So, if you are trying to do things the right way and "make money" for the assholes from

---

[42] Tolentino, Cierra. "Who Invented Math? The History of Mathematics | History Cooperative." *History Cooperative*, 6 Oct. 2023, historycooperative. org/who-invented-math/.

the previous chapter, the right thing to do is to have low-enrolled classes taught by adjuncts.

There are two kinds of low-enrolled courses. There are those that are just not super appealing to the student body due to the time of day or day of the week they are offered. I know a guy who always scheduled himself a course that met on Monday, Wednesday, and Friday from 8-8:50 in the morning. He didn't pick a super exclusive, upper-level course to schedule at this time; he scheduled a required course. One hundred percent of the students need to take this course before they graduate. He knows this. Yet he puts it on those days at that time. He has done it for years and years, and he gets away with it because he hoards the schedule. If I did his schedule, that shit would end.

Do all of those college students who have substance abuse problems want to get up and sit in a class at 8 in the morning three days a week? They do not. Will they be more inclined to take one that meets at that same time one day per week? Yes. They will. So what is the incentive to offer a class that early in the morning three times per week? It will always be low enrolled, but it will have just the right amount of students in it to hit the break-even point. Meanwhile, at noon on Tuesday and Thursday, an adjunct is teaching the same class with 30 students.

The other kind of low-enrolled courses are those above-mentioned specialty courses. These are courses that are exclusive to the folks who major in that field. The general rule is that if the course starts with a 3 or 4, it means it is a specialty course for majors only. There will be some courses at that level that are required for all graduates. They are generally senior seminar classes that are designed to tie the whole degree together, and everyone takes them, but for the most part, if the course is, say, History 319: Appalachia in the 1730s, there are only a select few history nerds in that class. They should take that course, but depending on the size of the school, there might only be a few people who are majoring in history. The bigger the school, the more majors. If this is a big state school with 60K students, this course is fine. A full-time teacher should teach it every year. It will always have 20 students in it. Great.

One of the places I worked had a professional administrator who handled the schedule. She was amazing at the job. She studied trends of when classes were filling and when they were not. She focused on the students' needs and made a schedule that reflected those needs. Then, and only then, did she assign people their classes. Now if that sounds like a brilliant way to go about it, then you have a good ear for brilliance, and you likely don't work at a university. In my 30 years of working in this field, I've worked as a full-time or adjunct faculty member at 8 different colleges and universities, and only one of the departments in one of the schools did this student-centric approach to scheduling.

Of course, the people who had seniority were scheduled first, and if they were willing to teach at a popular and useful time, they could have the same schedule all the time. That generally meant they were willing to teach four days per week for four hours per day. Popular times for traditional-aged college students are mid-morning and early afternoon twice per week. Non-traditional "adult" learners who are coming back to school like to have courses that meet early evening once per week or totally online. So, if someone was willing to make some "personal sacrifices" for the common good and teach full courses that run every time without question, that person could teach classes that meet from 10-12 and 1-3 Monday through Thursday with the hour between classes serving as "office hours" where they sit alone in their office eating lunch before the next class. They would likely have one day per week where they had a meeting that went from say 3-4, and that would be that.

That sounds pretty amazing, right? Well, I mean, unless the person doesn't want to teach full classes and do the work they were hired to do, then that sucks, but of course, that was why that department had the scheduler. All the courses were going to be at times that made sense for the students. What a concept.

However, this isn't the case at small schools. If there are only 1000 students, then there are likely only 7 or 8 history majors. Thus, courses like that one are only offered once every four years so that it is at maximum capacity. If you are a history major, you must take 319 when it is offered no matter what, or you will not graduate. That is the class to start at 8 in the morning three days per week. While the person who has the full-time job really, really wants to teach that Appalachia in 1730s class (spoiler alert, white people fight with Native Americans and say it is because God told them to do it), it makes no financial sense for that person to teach it because of the pay disparity. The adjunct who makes next to nothing should teach it.

If a full-time person teaches only these low-enrolled courses, then the adjuncts are exploited even more because they are being paid 2500 bucks per 30 students, which works out to 83 bucks per student and the full-time person is being paid 7500 bucks for 8 students, which works out to 937 dollars per student. It also means that when it comes time to cut programs, the one that is hemorrhaging money like that will be the first to go. Then those 8 history majors won't come to the school anymore because there will be no history department. That means those 8 students won't take any of the 24-30 non-major classes they needed to take to graduate, which means fewer sections of that required course, which means there isn't even 2500 bucks for an adjunct.

This sounds extreme, but it happens all the time. It is happening right now on every small campus in the country. The best case scenario is that the department folds and the full-time faculty are retained to only teach those lower-level required courses. They are called core courses, gen-ed requirements, or and this is true, the liberal arts requirements (That is three distinct ways of using that term for those keeping track at home). It sucks for the adjuncts who have put their heart and souls into teaching, but they sort of knew they were disposable even if they didn't read the first book in this series.

The worst-case scenario is that too many of these low-enrolled courses are taught by full-time faculty members, and the school loses so much money that it just collapses on itself. To repeat myself here, this sounds extreme, but it happens all the time[43]. It happened last year and the year before. It is happening right now.

[43] Moody, Josh. "A Look Back at College Closures and Mergers." *Inside Higher Ed*, 21 Dec. 2023, www.insidehighered.com/news/business/financial-health/2023/12/21/look-back-college-closures-and-mergers-2023.

I want to be an honest narrator and guide and state for the record that not every closure is the fault of gluttonous or slothful faculty. Some are the fault of greedy executives, but mostly it is a combination of all three. While book three of this trilogy will get into complex solutions as to how to save higher education from itself, the easy solution is right in front of us. It takes someone who has the willpower to use portion control when in charge because when a gluttonous hoarder is in charge, everyone is fucked.

I mentioned that non-traditional, adult degree-completion students prefer to have classes that meet one night per week or totally online. Well, by manipulating this schedule, people can and do end up working two full-time jobs at two colleges within driving distance of each other. I know that sounds like a crazy concept because I've gone out of my way to show how fucking lazy some people are. Why would they want to have two full-time jobs? That sounds like a lot of work.

For a normal, hard-working, student-oriented teacher, it would be super hard. I know because as a full-time adjunct, I did a lot of work for almost no money. There were times I had the teaching load of two full-time faculty members. Of course, I didn't have any of the other things to worry about. No meetings. No Steve. Fucking Steve. No bullshit. In. Teach. Out. Forget where I parked. Drive to the next place. Repeat. There is a whole book about this already. I won't linger. The point is that for a lazy, lust-filled, greedy, gluttonous fucking fuck face, two full-time jobs are maybe the same amount of work as one adjunct.

So, yeah, cards on the table in the spirit of full transparency, as a full-time faculty member, I do freelance. A lot of people do it[44]. I teach as an adjunct at other schools. I write books. I do some course design work. All of those things are to supplement my income because I don't make enough, and I work really hard. Most adjuncts, not the full-time adjuncts who are trying to work their way through the Academic Inferno, use adjuncting as a side hustle. They see the low pay as a bonus for a few hours per week.

---

[44] Woodward, Vivienne. "Why Your College Professor Has at Least One Other Side Job - Good.", 18 May 2017, www.good.is/money/contigent-faculty-not-paid-living-wage. Accessed 8 June 2024.

I don't love that attitude, but I understand it when we are only paying someone 70 bucks per student.

What I don't do and won't do is take a second full-time job and then do them both poorly. However, it happens, and the reason it can happen is because the person in charge puts himself in a schedule that allows him the freedom to do this. Maybe one of the full-time jobs is totally online and the other is in person. Maybe one is a small liberal arts college, say, an hour from his house, and the other is at a local community college. I say maybe, but I know this one has happened. I know because I received a call from an adjunct who told me that she would no longer be "allowed" to teach for my school due to the fact that her school instituted a non-compete clause once it was discovered that the head of one of the departments at her small, liberal arts college was busted for having a second full-time job. Thus, no one would be allowed to teach, even in the summer, which was when she normally taught at my school.

What is the difference between what I do, what that adjunct did, and what my adjuncts do? First, we are transparent about it. Everyone at work knows I am a writer. They know I do this other work. I get to teach courses and design courses that my school doesn't offer. I essentially teach the same two classes year-round, and while I like those courses, and I do my best to keep them from being stale, sometimes, I want to teach something else. I always put my full-time job first. I don't blow off a meeting at one school to go to a meeting at another school. It is truly supplemental income, and I do it because it is fun and a creative outlet. I didn't work my ass off to get through all the bullshit to become some lazy fuck who stuffs his load with bullshit classes or who pretends to do two full-time jobs when I am not doing anything but holding down a chair and collecting double the checks. I'm just a hard worker; I'm not a glutton.

LUST

No further may ye go
Ye holy souls,
Until the fire have burned you

Dante's Purgatory Canto XXVII

THE PRACTICE OF HAZING GOES BACK TO THE military in ancient Greece, so it makes perfect sense that it was the Greek organizations in higher education that started the practice. Research finds that the first reported incident of hazing in the United States happened before it was a country. In 1657, there was an incident of hazing at Harvard[45]. Harvard: spanking your ass since the 17th century. Wait, what? How does hazing have anything to do with lust? Again, not doing research into BDSM, but I do have some hot takes.

We think of hazing often from the perspective of the perpetrator as the bully and the victim as, well, the victim. We should. It is a vindictive, fucking fucky thing to do. I almost kept describing things there. I went on for a while, but fucking fucky does the trick. People who haze others were, at one point, hazed themselves. Did they like it? Maybe? Odds are, though, they found it humiliating. That is what hazing is. It is a process by which people in power require people not in power to do horrific things to prove their loyalty or their worth. What if, and hear me out, instead of doing that, we just took people at their word and judged them by the work they do? No? Hmmm. My bad.

---

[45] Lehman, Alexandra. "A Brief History of Fraternity/Sorority Paddles and Recommendations." *Fraternal Law*, fraternallaw.com/newsletter2/a-brief-history-of-fraternity-sorority-paddles-and-recommendations.

I am not victim-blaming here. Let me be clear. I am not victim-blaming. I am not victim-blaming. For real. However, I do need to spend some time looking at this from the victim's perspective, why they put up with this stuff, and more importantly for the sake of this chapter, how lust plays a part. Seriously though, hazing is bad, and it should be stopped. People should go to Stop Hazing dot Org[46] and read and get involved.

Remember, not victim-blaming.

There are wants and there are needs. Maslow's Hierarchy of Needs[47] tells us that we need our physiological needs (food, clothing, shelter) first. After that, we need security in the form of a job or property. Something tangible that we can call our own. Above that is love and belonging. That is where friendship, family, and being connected come into play. Higher up the ladder is self-esteem followed by self-actualization. I'm not going too much further into this. If you want more, plenty of colleges are teaching psych classes right now. I am sure my school has room.

The word I want to focus on here is "belonging." Love is easy to get. Want to be loved? Get a dog. They are love machines. Sure, they are high-maintenance, but love pours out of them at every turn. I know having a dog isn't the same as having a life partner, child, or best friend, but at some point, the people we love need us to clean up some of h/i/r bodily fluids for h/i/m. Dogs are just more honest about it. It's the lack of speech or thumbs that gets them into a bind. Belonging is hard. Falling in love is hard. Making friends is hard. Raising children is hard. Worth it, for sure, but hard. Getting a dog is pretty easy. Thus, love isn't all that difficult. Love is as easy as being licked in the face.

Belonging, though, that is a kick in the balls. People want to be accepted. People want to be loved. According to some 90's Britpop[48] songs, they might even want to be adored. I know some

---

[46] "StopHazing | Leading Resource for Hazing Research and Prevention." *Stophazing.org*, stophazing.org/.

[47] McLeod, Saul. "Maslow's Hierarchy of Needs." *Simply Psychology*, 24 Jan. 2024, www.simplypsychology.org/maslow.html.

[48] StoneRosesVEVO. "The Stone Roses - I Wanna Be Adored (Official Video)." *YouTube*, 25 Oct. 2009, youtu.be/4D2qcbu26gs?feature=shared. Accessed 8

people may argue that having kids is about belonging, but anyone who has been a parent or a child, so, you know, everyone, knows that isn't true. Kids don't always feel like they are part of the family, and parents can feel rejected by their kids. Belonging is never given in any relationship, and so people accept being hazed because s/he/y knows, as s/he/y can see from the results of the people who are doing the hazing, if one suffers through this pain and humiliation, then one gets to be part of the team/fraternity/sorority, or unfortunately, the college department.

While there is some research on this topic, most of the stories one finds about faculty hazing are personal. There are books and articles to be sure, but I can't seem to find a lot of credible, longitudinal studies because the people doing the hazing don't want the tea spilled and the people who've been hazed are afraid to spill the tea because they think that the only way to keep the jobs they've worked so hard to earn while suffering the humiliation is to keep their mouths shut.

See, hazing breaks us down from the inside. While in extreme circumstances, hazing is physical pain; in academia, it is something different. It breaks our spirits. It is abusive, mind-altering behavior. When one is hazed, one can, not always, but often, feel that one deserves the treatment. "Oh, Sally is being a huge bitch to me. It is my fault because I disagreed with her in that meeting. Oh, Steve is sending me veiled threats via email. My fault for daring to say "no" to his stupid idea." OK, yes, those are actual names of actual people who bullied me. While I use "Steve" as a theoretical fuck face, he was and is an actual person who is a fuck face.

I did try to lodge complaints with my supervisors on both of them, and it went badly. With Sally, I was told that my union didn't have anti-bullying policies because, and this is true, the union leadership wouldn't bring it up for a vote because it would likely pass. With Steve, I was told he was just a "sour puss," and we should just leave him alone and ride him out until he retires. For real. I was told, "Be hazed and accept the bullying" because... reasons.

While I took the abuse, I didn't participate in the culture of hazing. I wanted the job, but I didn't lust for the things they thought I would. I didn't desire it so much that I was willing to eat unsalted shit with a smile. For me, and this is the case for some of my colleagues, we eat the unsalted shit because this is the job we want. No job is perfect, but we love this job. We are in the service industry. We consider what we do teaching. We don't think we are in the "Ivory Tower." We often try to do good work while focusing on the students. We reluctantly take promotions when we see there is a chance to use the promotion for good, not because it helps us personally.

However, because so many people want so much more, they want to not only be in the Ivory Tower; they want to be at the top. They know that the further up they go, the more power and control they have. As we know from the previous chapter, they have the chance to control the schedule for themselves, but they also want to control the schedule so they can use it for blackmail.

I mentioned that even at the school where the schedule was done by an impartial professional, there was a seniority process for filling it in. That is right. I believe in earning one's place. However, when the person in charge is a Sally or a fucking Steve, then seniority doesn't matter. Rank doesn't matter. Time in the barrel doesn't matter. Nothing matters but how much ass one kissed and how much shit one took.

It is easy to lust after that sweet 16-hour workweek. Many a young faculty member, fresh out of the Inferno and standing on the seemingly solid ground of Purgatory Mountain, will jokingly ask, "Who do I have to blow to get that schedule?" The answer is, of course, Steve, and he will remind you of it pretty quickly. I'm not saying he walks around literally with his dick out asking for it to be sucked, but his fly is open, and his drawers are metaphorically down. How does he know to do it? Well, because if we look closely at his knees, we see the indentations from his time on the floor blowing whomever he had to blow when he first got there.

Instead of being disgusted that the academic version of the casting couch was alive and well, he dropped to his knees and did what he thought needed to be done. Then, when the fresh fish came along, he slid to the side and got to be close pals with his tormentor. To be fair, he could fucking hate that person. Odds are he did and does, but you can't un-suck a dick. Besides, that amazing 16-hour workweek is within reach, and eventually he will be the one in charge, and someone else will do what "needs to be done."

It isn't just a schedule that people lust for; it is so much more. The person in charge of a department or division has the power to give out offices and assign people to committee work and the ever dreaded: "other duties as assigned." Yeah. My contract has an open-ended, "other duties as assigned" clause at the end of it. This is a pretty standard practice in higher ed. I am not sure if it plays everywhere, but I assume it does. I know plenty of women (Let's face it. It is almost always women) who, as executives, get the coffee or order lunch. It can't just be the breast thing because there are plenty of dudes in the C-Suite who need some extra support on top.

More on those "other duties" in a bit. For now, let's whack the low-hanging fruit: office space and committee work. The reason that Mike Judge's *Office Space*[49] works so well is that, regardless of one's industry, there is something that rings true there. Of course, he goes over the top to prove a point. Still, when Ron Livingston takes the cubicle apart and pushes it down, or when the "heroes" take a printer to a field and smash it to bits while "Die Motherfucker (Still)" plays, those moments are pure wish fulfillment. We all know that we need some privacy, and we need our equipment to work.

Open offices are the Devil's work and reminiscent of the Panopticon[50], a punishment theory that places one central eye in the center of a prison with the idea that there is nowhere to hide, so inmates will be on their best behavior as they can, in theory, be watched at every second. Am I being a bit hyperbolic here? Cubicles are not prisons. That is true, but the feeling of constantly being watched leads to one feeling judged at all times, which can lead to persecution. Did I mention there are openings in my college's psych courses? We even offer them online; they can be taken from anywhere at any time.

---

[49] Judge, Mike. *Office Space*. 1999. 20th Century Fox.

[50] The ethics centre. "Ethics Explainer: The Panopticon - What Is the Panopticon Effect?" *THE ETHICS CENTRE*, 18 July 2017, ethics.org.au/ethics-explainer-panopticon-what-is-the-panopticon-effect/.

I've had offices, and I've had cubes. Since everyone agrees the cubes suck Steve's sweaty balls already, why not do just a little bit more and get the reward? The thing is, even with cubes, someone has an office. There may be a glass door, but there is a door. It closes. People can't walk behind that person and see what s/he/y is doing on the computer nor can anyone hear every word of every conversation s/he/y has on the phone. If the person in charge is giving out the offices, not based on merit but favoritism, what is a little indignity now for years of privacy? What the people forget is that the blackmail doesn't end. Getting the office and keeping the office are different things. Lust is MUCH stronger when one knows what the good stuff is. Every addict everywhere knows. The first hit is good, but the second hit is not as good, yet it feels essential. Hits three through infinity are no longer wants but needs. Where the fuck is my coffee/cigarette/bump/privacy? Whom do I have to blow to get it?

The same goes for committee assignments. Like offices or office spaces, some are way better than others. In higher ed, most full-time faculty serve on one or two committees. This is called "shared governance" by some and "exploitation" by others. The truth is somewhere in between. Committees are generally groups of faculty, executives, and staff who meet monthly (or more) to do the work of the institution. The staff who are included on these committees are the non-teaching, non-executive employees who have an academic adjacent role. Public safety and food service folks are not invited, although sometimes the decisions that are made in committees affect them.

Some of these committees meet several times per month and do a lot of work that pisses people off. The curriculum committee is the one people hate the most because those are the folks who decide if the new class you want to teach is going to be approved or not. Often the answer is no, and that pisses people off. Being on the curriculum committee is not a pleasant experience. In police movie terms, being on the CC is like being in IA, Internal Affairs: cops who investigate other cops. Other committees that suck are the academic standards committee, the faculty senate, or anything that involves oversight over a colleague. Maybe if cops weren't dirty or if faculty wrote good classes, then there wouldn't be a problem, but people are the worst.

The best committees are the ones where people sit around and talk and/or hand out money. Yeah. That is real. There are committees whose whole purpose is to give people promotions, to give out grants, or to talk about the rules. These committees often only meet a few times per year and don't need to show a lot of results. The people who apply for promotions or grants do the work, the rules never change, but they need to be "considered" forever and ever. The people in power give out these committee assignments, and people lust after the easy, sit-around bullshit assignments, so once again, there is a lot of ass-kissing complete with reach-arounds.

If the bad office or the bad committees doesn't deter one or break one down, the final power play is to use the "other duties as assigned" clause. Here, in no particular order, are some duties I've been assigned. I was "asked" to teach a class I'd never taught before with one day of preparation. I was "asked" to be on a search committee during a paid break. I was "asked" to revamp curriculum for no pay. I was "asked" to attend a meeting hundreds of miles away without reimbursement for time or miles. I was "asked" to speak at a conference but was "told" I had to pay for my food while I was there. I was "asked" to give a professional development presentation on a topic I knew quite a bit about, but I was "told" to use the material provided to me and NOT to veer from it.

The list is much longer than that. I will stop there. There is no end to the things people can be "asked" to do. These things often involve not only the loss of time for no pay, but also cost the person money or dignity or both. The more you come into conflict with the person in charge, the more duties will be assigned. It is an ugly truth, and it happens all the time.

There are, of course, other duties that are assigned that involve time off, trips with pay, or both. Some duties might be to present a paper, co-write an article for publication, or spend some grant money on a special project that is sure to only benefit a small group of people. Those things sound awesome, and they are, and it is obvious why people lust for them.

The truth is power can be like a light to moths. They will line up to get as close to it as possible because it feels good. They lust for warmth and comfort. There are often a bunch of other moths close to that light, and so there is companionship there too. That light is so bright and good, and they just really, really want it, and unfortunately, they don't know it is a bug zapper until it is too late.

THE EARTHLY PARADISE

I left the edge,
And entered very slowly

Dante's Purgatory Canto XXVIII

AS WE APPROACH THE END OF THIS COLLECTION,

I would be remiss to mention again, in case it hasn't been obvious, that this book is a classic middle. Like the middle story of the original *Divine Comedy,* middle stories are bridges to the big finish. Think *Empire Strikes Back, The Two Towers,* or *Back to the Future II*. Each of those end with the heroes having had the shit beat out of them in some way, having barely survived, but they feel ready to run headlong into the final battle. They end in defeat, someone loses, something is lost, but the next thing, the big finish, will make it all right again.

My time in Purgatory, which felt like forty lifetimes, is over. I've climbed that mountain and come through the muck, and now, like Dante, who in the real book leaves Virgil behind for the finale, I've made some hard choices to get here. I'm now back on Earth, looking at a lush green paradise, and I am living the dream.

Okay, I wouldn't say that I'm living *the* dream, but I am living my dream. All I've ever wanted was to be a teacher. I got into a heated argument with someone once when I said, during my early years of teaching when I was still lost in the woods and could have gotten out of limbo if I wished, that all I wanted was for each of my students to think big thoughts. Sure, I wanted them to be able to write better or become better researchers or whatever I was supposed to do as an English teacher, but what I cared about was that they had original thoughts and considered things they hadn't considered before.

I was just being honest and vulnerable with a person whom I thought would understand, but instead, she laughed. Laughed a real laugh *at* me. She thought I was being idealistic and stupid. My job, as she saw it, was just a job. It was to make money for myself and my family. I was there to get students out of school so they could get jobs. I was a replaceable cog.

It hurt quite a bit. It still bugs me to think about that. Still, I understand what she was saying. Most people are cogs. Most people are replaceable. Most things people do have no meaning whatsoever. The reason that those things have no meaning has nothing to do with what they do. It all comes down to how they do it.

I'm not a cog because I don't want to be a cog. I don't want to be a lazy, greedy, vengeful teacher. Thirty years later, and I still just want my students to think big thoughts. During the week that I wrote this chapter, I had a 90 minute virtual meeting with a student. She was struggling big time. The material wasn't dense, but she was stressed out. She had some personal stuff going on that was getting in the way of her being able to learn. So, we met. We talked. I asked a lot of questions about things that didn't seem to be connected to the assignment, but by the time we were done, I could come back to her answers and connect them to the assignments in a personal way. We hung up, and she was back on track.

She isn't an English major. Hardly anyone is anymore. Still, everyone has to take a writing class. I don't make future English majors; I help future nurses, engineers, accountants, historians, or whatever else someone wants to be, reach their goals. I am part of their journey, and while I know some of them have hated me (I've done my best to not look, but Rate My Professors is right there), I can sleep at night knowing that I've done my best by them every time. I tell them I am their mirror. I will work as hard as they work. I've done that for 30 years, and I plan on doing it for 30 more.

My pediatric dentist hated children. He hated me. He told me I was being hysterical for freaking out when he wanted to stick a needle into the roof of my mouth. I saw the needle. I understood how big my head was. I thought the needle was going to go into my brain. I didn't know that the whole needle wasn't going in and that the reason it was so long had everything to do with the size of the space between the plunger and my gums. He could have explained that to me, but instead, he got pissed and stormed off and went to get my mother to calm me down.

Lots of people have had bad experiences in the dentist chair or with a bad nurse who missed a vein while drawing blood or putting in an IV. Right now, someone who works at a grocery store is being a huge dick to an old lady who just doesn't know how to use the credit card reader. Some chef somewhere is getting an order wrong, not because she made an honest mistake, but because she doesn't care. Some car salesman is calling a customer "slick." Some teacher is finally returning papers without giving any feedback on them, three weeks after the due date.

Every one of those experiences is leaving a bad impression. Those mean, hurtful, disingenuous, and outright thoughtless acts will ripple out. It could be direct, and the lady will leave the grocery store and go home and yell at her neighbor. That could be bad and lead to someone having a broken nose or a busted hip. The lasting damage will be when the next time that woman goes to a store, or a dentist's office, or anywhere really, and feels unsure of herself, she will likely not ask for help or speak up on her behalf. While it may not have major repercussions, she may not tell the pharmacist that she feels bad when she takes those two medicines together, and she ends up having an allergic reaction that lands her in the hospital. I know that sounds extreme, but actions have consequences.

Every shitty, lazy, greedy teacher damages higher education. Every time a political leader shits on what we do and spits out the word "elite" with venom, even though he went to two Ivy League schools, another small liberal arts college shuts down. Every time a professor says, "I don't have time for you," a student drops out and never comes back while being saddled with student debt and NOT having a degree.

While I know it isn't perfect, and there are days when I think about getting a job as a custodian because while I know that I'll just have to mop that floor again tomorrow, I can see it clean for a moment, and most importantly, I can leave the work behind. Because I care so much, I never leave work at work. I'm sitting on a Sunday afternoon writing this book because I think my work is important, and I want to point out the flaws to help make it better. I've answered student emails before the sun came up today, and I will spend several hours tomorrow, a national holiday, grading assignments.

I've been teaching for 30 years. Because I teach year-round, I can say with confidence that I have at least 250 students per year come through my classes. It is likely more, but let's use that number. I do my best to connect on some level to every single one of them. I fail all the time, but I try to connect and ask them to think big thoughts and try big things. That means I've had at least 7,500 students sit in my classroom. Some of them have been virtual, but I am going to say they sat in my classroom anyway. If the Dunbar[51] number is real, then each of those people has 150 people in their lives with whom they are close enough to be part of that person's sphere of influence. That number is now 1,125,000. I am not taking into account the number of people those folks come into contact with every single day, but that means because of the way I do my job, I am two degrees of separation from over one million people's lives.

I also consider the fact that about 500 of those 7,500 students of mine are now teachers. They have hundreds of students per year who have a sphere of influence too. That multiplier goes on and on forever. I am not foolish enough to think that I have moved one million people to action, but I could have. I do the job every day as though I could. I take the job seriously. It is about me, but it isn't about me.

Wounds only heal when they are exposed to fresh air. We can keep them covered up, but that only allows them to fester. I want to show the world the gashes and talk about the ugliness. I want to get people talking about the flaws in the system so we can make it better. We can't let the fucky fucks win. I know it is an uphill battle, but it isn't a Sisyphean task. The boulder will rest at the top of the

---

[51] "New Study Deconstructs Dunbar's Number (Number of Friends)." *ScienceDaily*, www.sciencedaily.com/releases/2021/05/210504211054.htm.

mountain because I refuse to believe it won't. I'm proof that the system works.

I was a kid who found a way to a better life through education. Going to college and going into debt was worth it for me because I earned the degree which landed me the adjunct job, which allowed me to work for 17 years to land a full-time job. While I complain, and I will never stop complaining and fighting and pushing back and speaking truth to power, I believe that higher education needs to be saved. I believe that every community needs a college. I believe that the liberal arts make us better people.

In the final book of this series, I hope to show how things can change for the better. There are a lot of problems that I've addressed in these first two books for which I will offer solutions. Academia is full of people who say "Someone ought to…" and then they sit around and wait for someone to do that thing. I'm not that person. I am going to say, "Here is how I can…" and then I am going to try my damndest to make that thing happen. I am just one person, but I know I have a team of great people who will help. No one can do it alone, but it often takes one person to lead the charge.

The sad reality is that higher education is full of terrible monsters, and they have teams too. Villains have henchmen. The baddie gives the henchman power, money, drugs, whatever it is that person wants, and in exchange, the henchmen become the villain's backup dancers. Sure, every once in a while, the baddie is thwarted by someone who can't be bought, but s/he/y always finds a way to get back in power. I learned all about this as a child in this amazing docuseries from 1966 featuring Adam West, *Batman*.[52]

I know it seems like a stretch, but there is something about that show that rings true to academia. For whatever reason, in *Batman 66*, the commissioner and the chief of police are technically "in charge," and they supposedly can make changes. They are there to protect and serve while keeping the citizens of Gotham City safe. For some strange reason, they can't seem to figure out how to do the things they were hired to do.

They have a boss to whom they report, but he doesn't do much either. We don't see the Mayor much in that show. He is a guy

---

[52] *Batman*. Created by Lorenzo Semple Jr. and William Dozier. 1966.

called Mayor Linseed whose big job is to call the Commissioner, who, of course, calls Batman. He doesn't have a first name, but he is absolutely a white, douchey douchebag who is likely worried about staying in power and answers to the name Steve. I'm not saying he is corrupt, but he clearly isn't doing much to stop the madness. Would anyone doubt that he would take money from The Bookworm to help fund his re-election campaign? I mean…

Thankfully for them, and the citizens, there is one person who remains incorruptible and who has a few sidekicks and helpers who are willing to do the job without wanting the accolades. They don't need to be out in front. They don't want to be the face of the system. Re-election can leave that to Mayor Steve and Commissioner Gordon. They even wear costumes and have secret identities. They just want the system to work. They want to root out corruption. They do the work because they care, because it is right, and because they want to serve.

Holy Academic Shit.

I'm Batman?!

THE DIVINE COMEDY WILL CONCLUDE WITH...

ACADEMIC PARADISE

SAME BAT-TIME, SAME BAT-PUBLISHER

BOOK CLUB QUESTIONS

1. Have you ever heard the term "Ivory Tower" before this book?

2. What did you know and what did you think it meant?

3. Did you think that being a full-time Professor is a good job? How do you feel after reading this book?

4. Do you think Professors should be required to change what material they teach from year to year?

5. How should Professors dress when teaching? Why?

6. Do you think teachers' unions should be used for higher education? Why or why not?

7. Has your opinion of tenure changed since reading the second book in this trilogy?

8. What do you think of the current state of higher education?

9. Do you think a college degree has the same value now as before? Explain.

10. Do you think that it matters what type of higher education one has? Does a technical degree or a liberal arts degree have more value right now?

AUTHOR BIO

Virgil Henry

VIRGIL HENRY IS A SALTY PROFESSOR WITH 30 years of teaching experience in higher ed. He has taught thousands and thousands of students. He has some hot takes.

Discover more at
4HorsemenPublications.com

10% off using HORSEMEN10